TREASURES BENEATH OUR FEET

*A Selection of Historical Finds from the
Fields of England whilst Metal Detecting
over 30 Years*

Charlie Atkinson

This book is dedicated to my wife Annette who has spent most Sundays over these thirty years on her own! But I know she secretly enjoyed looking at some of the finds too.

Acknowledgements

I would like to thank the following for their help in assembling the information and some of the photographs used in this book.

Norwich Museum Services and Finds Liaison Officers in the 1990's For their understanding and promoting the use of Metal Detectors at that early stage whilst some areas were against the hobby.

Lincoln and Scunthorpe Finds Liaison Officers for their identification and allowing me the access to the national database and allowing me to use their data and photographs.

Wikipedia for enabling ordinary people to gain access to a vast amount of knowledge,data and photographs which enlightens so many people around the world.

Our Local Metal Detecting Club 'Lincoln Searchers' and all their members for the great days out in field where we are can relax, find some amazing historical items, have lunch together and discuss our finds and just laugh even in the worst weather possible. We must be mad!

Finally our Farmers and Landowners who trust us and give us permission to detect on their land knowing that we will in some cases share our finds with them or in other cases donate funds to a charity of their choice.

About the Author

Born and Bred in Lincoln, England, Charlie Atkinson is a lover of everything historical in his beloved country. He picked up metal detecting as a hobby in the '90s and took full advantage of having the ability to spend so much time exploring which areas would be the best to search for little parts of history that he could touch and show others. This is his first book to exhibit some of his most important finds in the past thirty years.

Contents

Author's Note

This is the story of one man's hobby over a period of 30 years.

Hello! I am Charlie Atkinson, born and bred in Lincoln, and attended schools there and in surrounding villages before settling down to a family life.

I have worked in Road Haulage for over 40 years starting as a Clerk and eventually a Transport Manager.

It was demanding work over many hours a week, so I was always looking for a hobby to take my mind off it for a while. Moving to Norfolk with my work gave me an opportunity that I was looking for…

In 1991, after 21 years in Road Transport and working as a Transport Manager in Norfolk following a move with my job from Lincoln, I was on call 24

Hours a day and desperately needed to be able to forget work for at least a day!

I lived in Mid Norfolk, close to a main route from London to Norwich, with my wife and son, and I really wanted a hobby that interested me.

One day, we got talking to our neighbours over the back fence, and he told me about how he and his wife would go to Gt Yarmouth to metal-detect on the sand most weekends. He was really enthusiastic about it and proceeded to show me a box of his finds from the beach. These included dozens of rings of Gold and Silver, brooches, bracelets, and necklaces. All the jewellery one could find on a beach or in the water whilst swimming or playing.

He also explained that they always found enough cash each time to pay for their fish and chips!

All the time he was explaining this to me, I was thinking that I could not do that; it was like waiting for everyone to leave and pick up a bit of their personal belongings!

But, I thought, If I could find some local land with a bit of history around it, that would be interesting!

So, after a quick lesson with their detectors, I set about looking for one that I could get used to or try out, without spending a fortune, because even in the early '90s, the most expensive detectors were over £1000 each. But first, I had to get permission from someone, and the easiest way was to walk around to the local farm and ask the owner if it would be possible. Then, I came to an agreement to share proceeds if I made any valuable finds.

So down the road, I went and drove down the long drive and over what looked like an old moat into the yard of this huge Elizabethan building; it was massive!

I admit I was a little wary about asking the owner of this huge hall if he would let me walk all over his land looking for relics!

However, I need not have worried; he and his wife were the most decent, reasonable people you could hope to talk to. I explained why I needed a hobby and what work I did, and he was really welcoming and said

I could go anywhere on his land as long as I didn't damage any crops.

He gave me a map of all his fields—there must have been over forty of them. I thought I was never going to cover all these, but at least I would have fun trying!

He did explain to me that he had some detectorists on his land before, but they never found anything! I soon found out that someone had been telling porkies!

I thanked them both for giving me permission and promised to keep them informed of any nice or unusual finds.

Then I went home a happy bunny and started looking for a metal detector.

We didn't have a computer back in the early '90s, so the only way to find a detector was to look in either Treasure Hunting or the Searcher Magazines. I ordered The Searcher from our local Newsagent and sifted through it, checking out what I thought I could afford. Not knowing whether I would even like the hobby, I plumped for a second-hand C-Scope Detector from

Joan Allen, along with some headphones and a digger.

I did not have long to wait before they arrived; however, as it was now winter, I had to invest in some warm, waterproof clothing and somewhere to put all my finds when I dug them up!

So fully kitted out, I rang the farmer and asked which field I could start on and off I went.

Let me tell you that within an hour, I found my first coin and musket ball.

For any person looking for a hobby where you can touch history and take history home and learn something new nearly every time you go out, this is the hobby for you!

I have never in all the 30 years of detecting gone home with nothing!

Saying that, I have taken kilos and kilos of rubbish from the fields, like lead and silver paper and plough shards, used shotgun cartridges, etc.

There is also the likelihood of finding things you wouldn't expect today, like objects from the Second World War, for example, live ammunition, which needs to be handled with care. Of course when you receive a good signal, everyone gets excited as to what it could be, but each signal needs to be carefully removed from the ground, just in case. If anyone does find live ammunition, then the authorities or the farmer or both, need to be informed to deal with it.

The main idea for this book covering the 30 years I have been detecting is not just to show you my best finds, but to document and exhibit the 50 finds from each decade that I have actually enjoyed finding for differing reasons. I will also explain, if I can, just why they are special to me—the first person to actually handle each item since the person who lost them for whatever reason. But they are all treasures to me.

I would also like to explain that everything I have found that I thought wasn't rubbish I have taken to the local finds liaison officer to log, identify and date them. Sometimes when cleaning, I have had a surprise or two and found something rare when I originally thought it was a bit of rubbish. Hence, it is always important to clean your finds, even if it looks like a bit of old lead!

Whilst in Norfolk, my finds were taken to Norwich

Castle Museum, where they were all sorted behind the scenes upstairs. It was a really exciting place to visit a few times a year.

Finally, you may have to forgive me for the quality of some of the photos. We cannot be good at everything, but I have improved over the years. I hope you find the first 50 finds interesting and it gives you the urge to join the thousands of detectorists in the UK and bring home some history! But before I show you these 50 items, I would just like to share with you what choice of items we still find today in the fields around Britain.

I could show you 50 coins or 50 artifacts, but you would soon get bored with that. I have found hundreds of musket balls and buttons, which are common finds. Another thing detectorists must remember is to obtain insurance; there are a couple of places you can obtain insurance, and it is best to check online for the best deal for you, which covers any accident whilst out detecting in the fields. This also impresses the Farmers when you show them your card, and it does not cost a lot either.

Once out in the fields, do not go on growing crops unless you have permission to do so!

When you find a target and remove it, take it out carefully and refill the hole, this way you will keep the farmer happy and keep him informed of all your finds. This will also ensure that you keep your permission intact. Don't give them any reason to stop you going on their land, because permissions are so hard to get, and farmers talk to each other.

I once found a complete bridle bit in a grass field, I cleaned it up, polished it, and took it to the farmer; he loved it and hung it up in the kitchen. It is small acts like this that help them trust you, because you do have to earn their trust. On the downside, one day I dug down over a foot in a grass field and pulled out a mortar bomb complete! I carefully put it down and rung the farmer; he arranged for the army to sort it out. I left the field in a state of shock, but it taught me a lesson in being careful whilst digging.

I find that researching the objects is just as rewarding as actually finding them, so if you decide to take up metal detecting, enjoy it for as long as you are able; it is indeed a fascinating hobby.

After persevering and enjoying the hobby for a year, I traded in the C Scope for a Fisher and found my find rates immediately improved! So, the adage proved correct—you get what you pay for, as with everything else in life!

My idea for this book is to show you what is still in the ground and display a variety of finds from each decade. In this edition, I would just point out that the finds are not in any order of importance or age, or even value. Enjoy!

Just a disclaimer, all information on these finds were given by professionals and if there are any errors in that information, I can only apologise in advance.

The 1990s

My 1st unusual find below is a bronze mould for making a lead shot or a musket ball! This mould dates from 1400-1800.

These do not come up regularly and are fairly rare finds, so it is an interesting find that I shared in the talks I gave at our local WIs (Women's Institutes).

Musket balls are common finds in the fields of Norfolk and I am one of the lucky people to have found a couple of hundred or so over the years of all different sizes from pistol balls to the largest being Brown Bess shot, I think, but I am not an expert on the subject.

Most of the musket balls found in the fields were from hunting rather than action I understand. But if you are lucky enough to have a battle site you will be kept very busy.

The earliest go back to the 14th century through to the 19th century so roughly 500 years of use.

When I take musket balls into the FLO Office, they still like to record them as some are over three hundred years old.

My 2nd item is one of many different bells I have managed to find over the years. This one was identified as a post-medieval rumbler bell with a fish scale design, and once cleaned it still rang!

I normally call them crotal bells but they could be either. Bells were originally made in two pieces. They were initially made in the 14th century but this type is more like the 16th-17th century, so still 400 years old and were fitted on animals like horses, cows and sheep. Some had the makers' marks on too which are rarer still. I once found four bells on one leather strap! They all rang too!

It is still nice to uncover one that still rings when cleaned!

My 3rd item is another rare one for us detectorists and it isn't that old either. Whilst I went around the county carrying out talks at the local WIs, I always asked if anyone knew what this could possibly be and no one ever got it right.

But then it wasn't until our FLO told me that I knew either!

This is a bull's nose ring from the 19th century according to those who know.

I couldn't help but wince when they told me, and thought the pain of having one of these ripped out of your nose, would bring tears to your eyes!

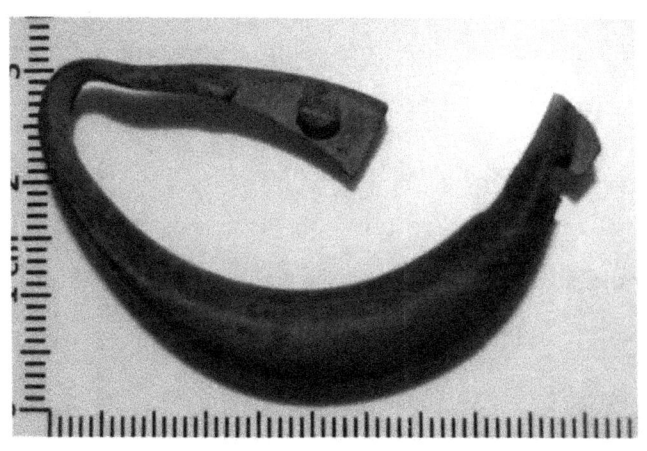

My 4th find is both unique to me and a rare find on the whole, not many people will have found one of these tokens.

A Bungay halfpenny copper token dated 1795.

On the obverse, it reads "For the Use of Trade" with justice standing on a pedestal.

On the reverse, it says, "We promise to pay the bearer on demand one halfpenny", with Bungay across the top and the date at the bottom.

Trade tokens were minted all over the country to give out as change not only by towns but also by individual businesses, these tokens could then be used to buy things in the future at the same place of purchase.

Tokens are really nice to find and there are hundreds of different ones in our soils.

This is a particularly good example.

9

My 5th find is a copper farthing of Charles II dated 1672.

Obverse: Carolvs .A. Carolo Above the left-facing head.

Reverse: Britan nia on both sides of Britannia, date below.

These coins are not uncommon but this one is a nice example. They normally come out of the ground either very well-worn or partially/fully corroded.

So to find a nice example like this is a very rare event.

These farthings were the first regal issues of copper coins to be struck at the Royal Mint, first issued in 1672. Previous copper coins had been struck under licence privately, or as tokens issued by local businessmen, and this was the first time Britannia appeared on British coins since Roman times.

For me, this was, and is, a very special coin to find.

My 6th find is a Roman bronze coin, not the first I found, but the first I found that had been pierced in antiquity by a Saxon and more than likely worn around their neck!

The coin itself, I was informed by Norwich Museum at the time is a bronze follis of Constantine dated 320-3 AD. Although it is very worn, as are most Roman Bronze coins when they are unearthed (if not totally corroded away with bronze disease) this has survived fairly well and must have been cherished by a Saxon for some reason, maybe even as a trophy?

To me, it shows that no matter what the people were like 1500 to 2000 years ago, they were not much different to us in certain ways!

13

My 7th find from the fields of Norfolk is another unfamiliar find for us detectorists and to me as a beginner at the time was something I thought looked a bit weird and I hadn't a clue what it was at the time.

It is an apothecary's weight made of bronze and dated to the Post-medieval period around the 18th century.

They were developed in sets of weights which were developed toward the end of the 17th century possibly by the Society of Apothecaries who held the contract to supply medicines to the Army and Admiralty which would include scales, weights, bandages and medications.

These weights didn't seem to replace any previous form, they just seemed to appear very quickly and became widespread until the early 19th century and the advent of commercial scales.

My 8th find is another rare trade token from a neighbouring town in Norfolk. This is a copper farthing token of Diss dating to 1669.

These private trade tokens were produced as a necessity due to a lack of regal coinage following the Civil War, when Charles I had been beheaded and a period of Commonwealth government under Oliver Cromwell and later his son Richard. The Monarchy was restored in 1660 when Charles II ascended to the throne. At the time these tokens were struck there had already been close to 20 years without small denomination regal coinage and it wasn't until 1672 before Charles II farthings and halfpennies were issued.

Tokens like these were minted in many towns around the country and given as change which could be reused to buy goods later.

As Diss was close to where I lived, this is a special little find for me.

My 9th Norfolk find is one of the smallest medieval hammered coins I have found, and it is no wonder that these were lost in the first place.

It is a silver farthing of Edward I Minted in London and dated 1279 by the Norwich Museum.

This little coin is in really nice condition and it hasn't been bent by the plough over the years, which many hammered coins are, or broken, as they are so thin.

Obverse: A trifoliate crown with ornaments between the fleurs surrounded by EDWARDVS REX

Reverse: LONDONIENSIS

This little coin is one of my favourite coins of this period due to its condition and size. It's a little worn in places but you would expect that with it being nearly 750 years old!

My 10th find from Norfolk is another coin from Edward I, this is a silver penny dated from 1279-1307, according to the specialists in Norwich.

Most people would take a look at this picture and wonder why would you pick this as one of your 50 finds and I will explain shortly.

This coin is in the same condition as probably one of many thousands of hammered coins that come out of the ground from this period.

Obverse: +EDW REX ANGL DNS hYb

Reverse: CIVITAS LINCOL

The Lincoln Mint was active between 1280 and 1281; since I was born and bred in Lincoln and this is the only coin I have ever found from this early mint, it is so special to me.

So to those who think it looks rubbish, it may do, but some of these finds are always special to someone!

My 11th find is another unusual item and many millions of people are not even aware of their existence. But to us detectorists, these are very nice to find!

This is a Medieval English Bishops head jetton dating from 1282 to 1288 AD. So from the time of Edward I.

Jettons come in many shapes and designs from mainly England, France and Germany, and they span several hundred years. This example is one of the earliest and rarest types.

Jettons were produced in copper alloy and used to perform calculations for accountancy. They were in use from 13th to 16th centuries.

I have to say that some of these are so ornate, that it beggars belief they were only used as counters effectively. But it does seem so, and some are a lot more valuable than the coins of the same period.

So they are very collectable and a lovely thing to find.

23

My 12th find is another of those that you just know that you will not find another!

This is an Edward the Confessor Cut farthing dated 1053-6 and one of the very few Anglo-Saxon coins I have ever found. It is classed as a pointed helmet type and I love it!

During Late Saxon and Medieval times, silver pennies were cut in half to make halfpennies, and half again to make fourth-things, which later became farthings.

Although a few are still being found today, these coins are still rare and sought after by collectors, so the better the condition the more valuable they are.

Rarity also adds to the value.

Once again the majority of the population is not aware of the processes of cutting pennies in half and quarters.

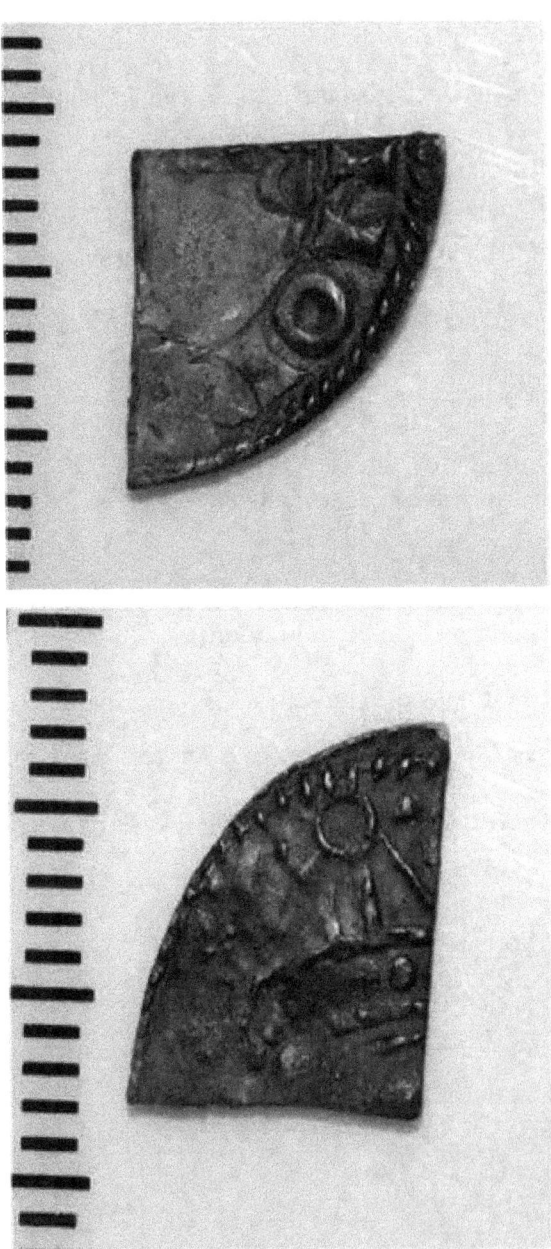

My 13th Norfolk find is another Hammered Coin, this time it is of Elizabeth I, it is a silver Penny dated from 1578-82 and it is not too bad a condition for a Lizzy coin, they are notoriously badly hammered, if you find a clear head on one of her coins, you do well.

Crowned bust facing left, initial mark crescent on both sides,

Obverse: E.D.G.ROSA SINE SINE SPINA (Although you can't see it all)

Reverse: CIVI TAS LON DON

Therefore Minted in London.

The Obverse Translation is "Elizabeth, by the grace of God, A Rose without a Thorn"

These pennies are so small, there is no wonder they were lost from people's purses.

Another of my favourite coins.

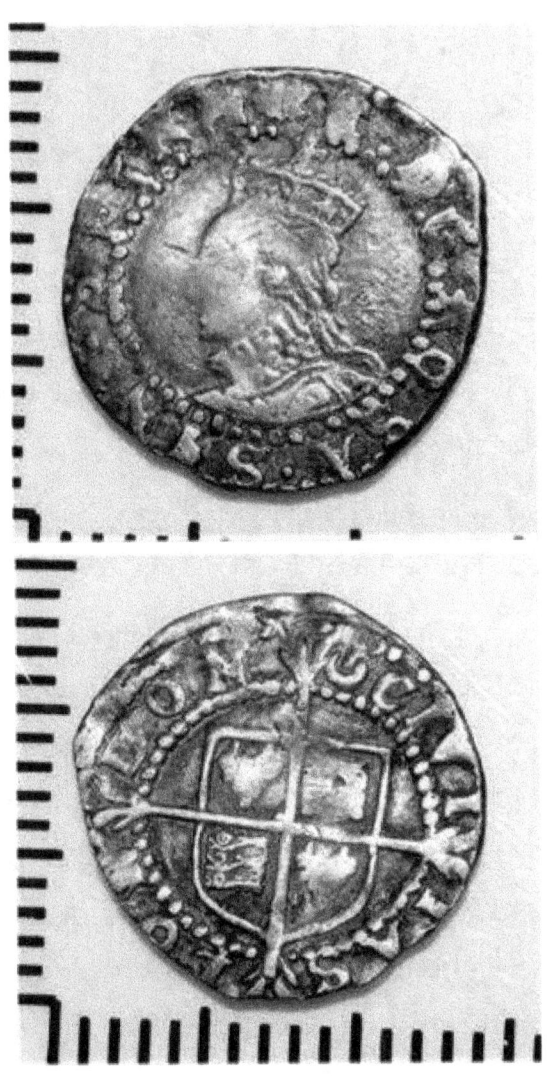

My 14th find is dated from the 1400s and is another jetton!

This time it is French and classed as a "Four Fleurs De Lis Lozenge" type.

Dated between 1415 and 1497 AD and made from copper, yet still in remarkable condition. These finds from this period are not very common at all, I don't expect to find another one like it.

The inscription around the Obverse translates to "Vive Le Roi" or Long Live the King.

There are lots of different French jettons found by detectorists and the condition of 95% of them are damaged as one would expect from the plough soil. So to get a nice one, in good condition like this is rare.

I have been lucky enough to find a few different ones from Norfolk, so I guess there must have been a trading site there at one time or a site for fairs or jousting contests between countries? Who knows?

My 15th find from the fields of Norfolk is one of the largest coins anyone would find anywhere, and boy do they give a great signal when you walk over them with a detector!

This is a George III Cartwheel Penny dated from 1797 and it is very unusual to find these in good condition.

The obverse shows the king's head facing Right, "GEORGIUS III .D.G.REX"

Reverse has Britannia with "BRITANNIA 1797"

These cartwheel pennies and the larger two pence were only minted until 1799 so you would expect not to find many in the soil.

In the early days, I found a few. But nowadays, as new land is hard to come by, very few seem to turn up.

This example is by far my best one, so very pleased with it.

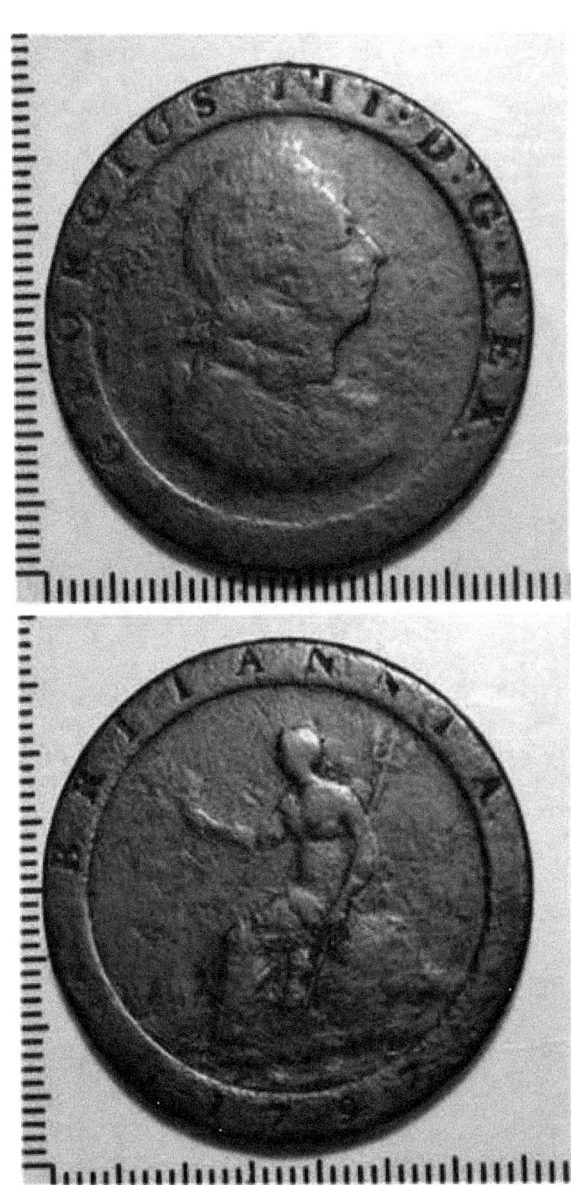

My 16th find from Norfolk is another unusual token, this time from Great Yarmouth. As with many tokens of the period, many come out of the soil worn and very fragile as they are very thin. Most of them are unreadable or cracked, so to find one complete is nice, to be able to read what is on them means they are rare.

This farthing dated from 1667 shows GREAT.YARMOVTH.1667 on the obverse.

The Reverse shows:

FOR.THE.VSE.OF.THE.POOR around the inner circle, a shield contains the city arms.

As with other tokens from local towns, these tokens were made/minted to improve the flow of money in trade in their local communities as there was very little small change available at the time.

These were given as change, so that they could be reused at a later date.

My 17th find is yet another token found in the Norfolk fields, this time it is worn but recognisable as a 1793 copper Hampshire D&H 11 Emsworth halfpenny Conder token.

As this token is more recent, the size and content of copper are more like the halfpennies of the Georgian period.

Obverse: Female seated left, right arm upon a globe and left upon an anchor, Denomination above, date in exergue. HALF PENNY 1793.

Reverse: Flying Dove and Cornucopia, "PEACE AND PLENTY" around the symbols.

Around the edge: "CURRENT EVERYWHERE"

This token is very worn, but to find it at all in Norfolk seems very weird!

It is very unusual and this is the reason for its inclusion in these first 50 finds, there is no way I will find another.

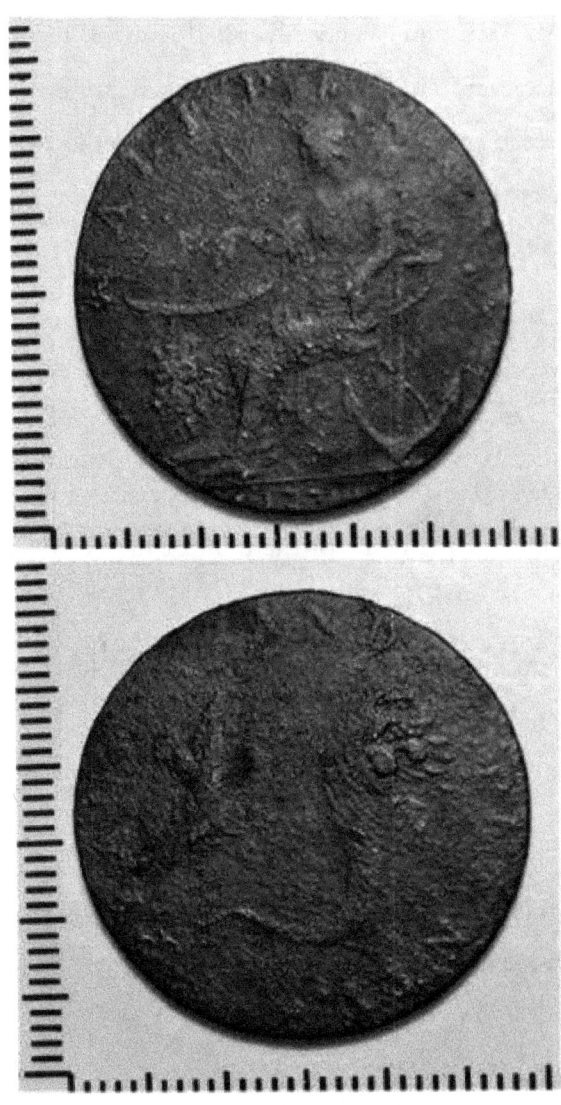

My 18th find is a cut silver halfpenny of Henry II. These coins are called short cross pennies as the crosses on the reverse are shorter than the pennies released later, which for obvious reasons were then called long cross pennies.

Cut halfpennies are quite common finds for detectorists but they are still nice to find and there are rare ones out there waiting to be found.

Dated 1180-9 AD this one, but because of the Cut, we can't see the name of the mint or the person who minted it.

The obverse would have read: HENRICVS.REX crowned facing bust holding sceptre,

Reverse would have shown the mint and who hammered it. It has 4 crosslets in each quarter.

This was one of my first cut halfpennies so this is why I included it in my 50 in this section.

My 19th find Follows on from the last one it is Henry II once again but this one is known as a "Tealby Penny" and these are notoriously known as being poorly minted, saying that. This is quite a good one in comparison to a lot I Have seen. These are not uncommon and do come up regularly but I wouldn't think many people have large collections of them.

Dated 1158-61 AD.

Obverse: HENRI REX ANG with face forward.

Reverse: Shows the mint and the name of the minter, in this case, it is Herbert of Winchester Mint.

The reason they are known as Tealby pennies is because a hoard of over 5000 of them was found at Tealby in Lincolnshire (my home county) in 1807.

Since then they have been called after that famous village. The coinage was so badly minted that the design and mints were all changed in 1180 when the Short Cross coinage was introduced.

The 20th find of these first ten years of my Detecting experience was, and is one of the best silver coins I have found. Other than being slightly bent and fairly well clipped by some naughty medieval people it is still a lovely coin.

This is a Groat (4 pence) of Henry VI Dated 1422-27 AD.

Obverse: Crowned facing portrait within beaded circle, royal title around.

hEnRIC DI GRA REX AnGL Z FRANC Translates to Henry by the Grace of god King of England and France

Reverse: Long Cross with trefoils in angles, 3 pellets in all angles, legend around in two circles. "POSVI DEVM ADIVTORE MEUM CIVITAS LONDON"

Translated to "I have made God my helper City of London".

Struck at the Tower Mint.

The daily salary of an archer in Henry V's army was four pence which increased to six pence in 1415. A gallon of the best ale cost 1.25 pence. A gallon of wine was four pence.

My 21st find in Norfolk is this rare and beautiful bronze ring. Well, it may not look it to you, but it is to me!

This is dated to the Iron Age therefore pre-Roman invasion 75BC-25 AD.

It isn't the first ring I ever found, but it certainly is the oldest.

I agree with those who may say that it doesn't look much, or it isn't very valuable! They are dead right on both comments. But I am never going to find another one!

These finds from pre-Roman times are nearly always a one-off!

I am very proud to say I found one of these, I wonder how many have been found since the '90s?

The problem with this one is that it already had the start of bronze disease when I found it, so I have to keep it at a steady temperature so it won't corrode away. If it's worth finding, it's worth looking after!

My 22nd find is once again a one-off, as I am not likely to find another one, It is a silver Shilling of James 1st dated 1603-4 AD.

Obverse: Head Facing Right "IACOBVS DG ANG SCO FRA ET HIB REX"

Translated to "James by the Grace of God King of England, Scotland, France and Ireland."

Reverse: Shield of Ireland "EXVRGAT DEVS DISSIPENTVR INMICI" which translates to "God Upholds the United".

This is one of the 1st Issues of Irish Coinage for James 1st and has the Bell mintmark Minted at the Tower Mint in London.

James succeeded Elizabeth I to the throne and reigned over the 4 Kingdoms for 22 years until he died in 1625.

45

My 23rd Norfolk find is my very first Penny of King John from my favourite Norfolk field.

This silver Penny dated 1205-10 AD is in good condition too, with slight wear on the face but no clipping from this coin.

This early coin from John's Reign was still hammered as Henry II his father.

Obverse King facing forward holding a sceptre. HENRICVS REX

Reverse RAVF ON LVNDE (RAVLF of London Mint)

John was considered a failure as a King as he lost a large amount of possessions inherited, In particular lands in France, like Normandy and Anjou. He surrendered his land to the Pope and faced a Baronial rebellion, a civil war and a war with France. He also lost his treasure close to the wash between Lincolnshire and Norfolk on his way to Newark where he died in 1216. So didn't seem to achieve much whilst on the throne other than agreeing and signing the Magna Carta! Nice coin though!

My 24th find of the '90s is one of my most valuable finds ever! It was found on the 7th May 1995 and I had only been detecting for 4 Years!

A Medieval Knights Solid Gold Seal Ring dated to the 15th century this ring was just sitting on the surface, glinting in the sun. I walked over to pick up what I thought was gold foil from a milk bottle. I picked it up, smiled to myself and went home. There was no way I was going to find anything else that day. My concentration would be totally shot!

I went and showed the farmer the following day, and as our agreement was that we shared everything over £50 Value at the time, we agreed for it to go to auction so I organised for it to go to Christie's in London. The entry in the catalogue is below the picture of the ring. There was no damage at all to the ring and we can only guess how it came to be in the field, but as some were worn on the outside of their gloves, our guess is he fell from his horse and lost the ring. Another once-in-a-lifetime find!

Today's value would be in excess of £20000. It was a lovely find and it fitted me too.

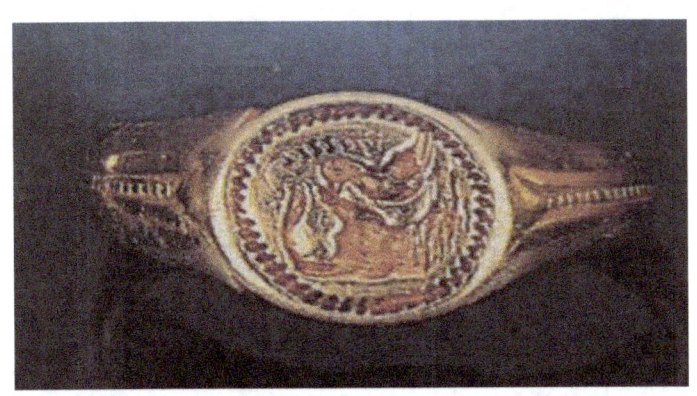

7   A LATE MEDIAEVAL MAGICAL SIGNET-RING

The circular bezel engraved with two lovebirds beside black letter inscription ? 'Trinit' in circular outer border, engraved at the back of the bezel *'Ananyzapta'*, the tapering hoop with pearled line
15th Century, finger size T ½

Provenance: Excavated at Attleborough, Norfolk

Cf. Oman, op. cit., 1974, nos. 74(a)(d) for two rings engraved with different versions of 'Ananyzapta'. The same inscription appears on the Middleham jewel. Cf John Cherry, The Middleham Jewel and Ring, The Yorkshire Museum, 1994, p.25 where it explains that the magical word 'ananizapta' was 'used as a charm against drunkenness or epilepsy, often known in the Middle Ages as the falling sickness'

$4,600-6,200   £3,000-4,000

After the Lord Mayor's Show, some would say we are back to what some would call basic detecting finds. But my 25th find is far from basic as it is a Late Bronze Medieval Sword Belt fitting from the 16th-17th centuries.

These fittings come in lots of different shapes and sizes, I guess it would be down to how much one could afford at the time.

I included it in the 50 as it is unusual to find one at all.

The value today of a fitting like this would be pennies similar to the value of bronze Roman coins today are 10 a penny unless they are complete and in good condition.

I found some examples exactly the same online so attached them to the same page, clearly my example was broken and maybe the reason for me finding it!

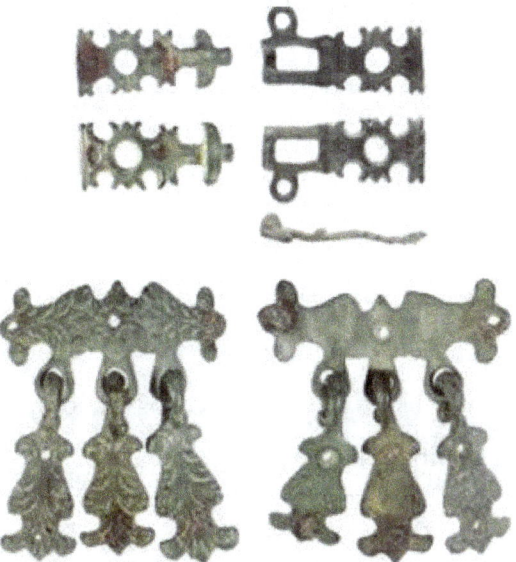

51

My 26th find from the 1990s is a Late Saxon Bronze Strap End.

As you can see this is a chunky piece of metal and a lot different to the majority of thin strap ends that come up from the Saxon and Viking era.

So it could possibly be more Medieval in date, but I am only stating what I have been told by the specialists. They have dated it 900-1100 AD.

As with the last item, there are hundreds of different styled strap ends surfacing each year from all different periods, the reason is that leather doesn't last very long, and they fell off!

So, a strap end is what it says on the tin, an end to a strap or belt.

There are some made from silver which can be valuable but from this age, they would become treasure and should therefore be reported to your local coroner. They are common but still nice to find.

53

My 27th find from Norfolk is a story within itself.

These are 75% of a full set of Iron Age Linch Pins from a Celtic Chariot from the Iceni Tribe (Boudicca's) 1st century BC/AD.

Made of bronze these pins held the wheels on the chariot, there was a bronze top (normally circular) and a bronze bottom (shaped like a horse's hoof) joined together with a piece of iron, which went through the axle the iron corroded over the years and Broke away and the wheel fell off.

Norwich Castle Museum informed me that I have proved to them that the chariot is still there in the ground and one day they may dig the rest up!

Because of the age and rarity of these, it was decided that it would be best for the Museum to have them and take care of them. It took 4 years to find these three items. I found the first top in my first year of detecting, so very special!

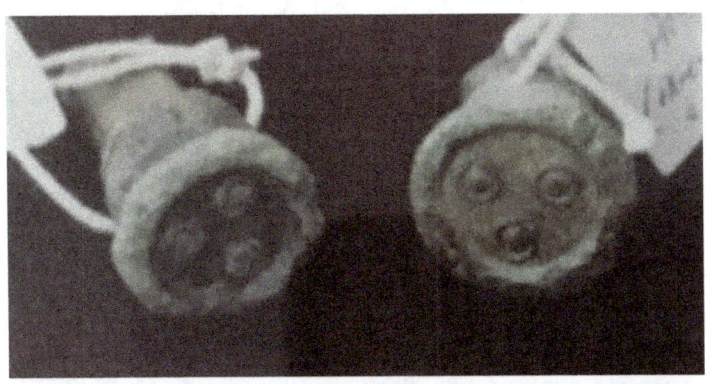

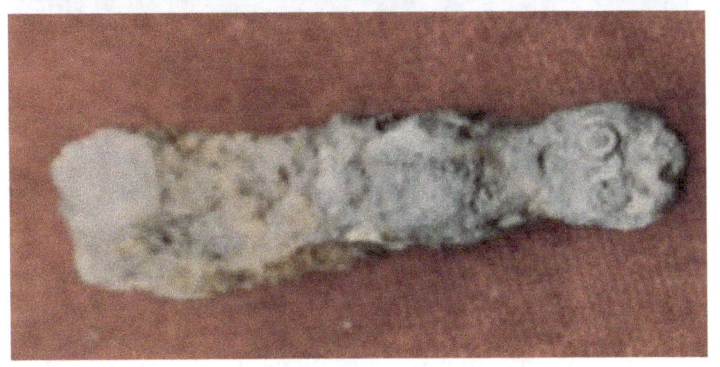

My 28th item goes back to the pre-Roman times too, probably the date not too far from the previous Linch Pins.

This is a Roman Legionary Denarius of Marc Anthony well known of course for his connection with Cleopatra, which gives a bit of context on the age of our finds. The date of the coin is from 32-31 BC, 70 years before the Roman invasion.

The obverse of all 39 different issuers shows a Roman Galley with an ornamental prow and a mast slanting forward, the legend reads "ANT AVG III VIR R P C".

The reverse on most issues shows an Aquila, the eagle standard carried by each legion between two standards, this one has Legio X Equestris.

The Legionary Denarii were the largest silver coinage produced in the late Republican Period. This was the oldest Roman Coin in my collection for 20 Years. Therefore regardless of it being worn, it is very special to me.

One to look out for in the fields of Britain.

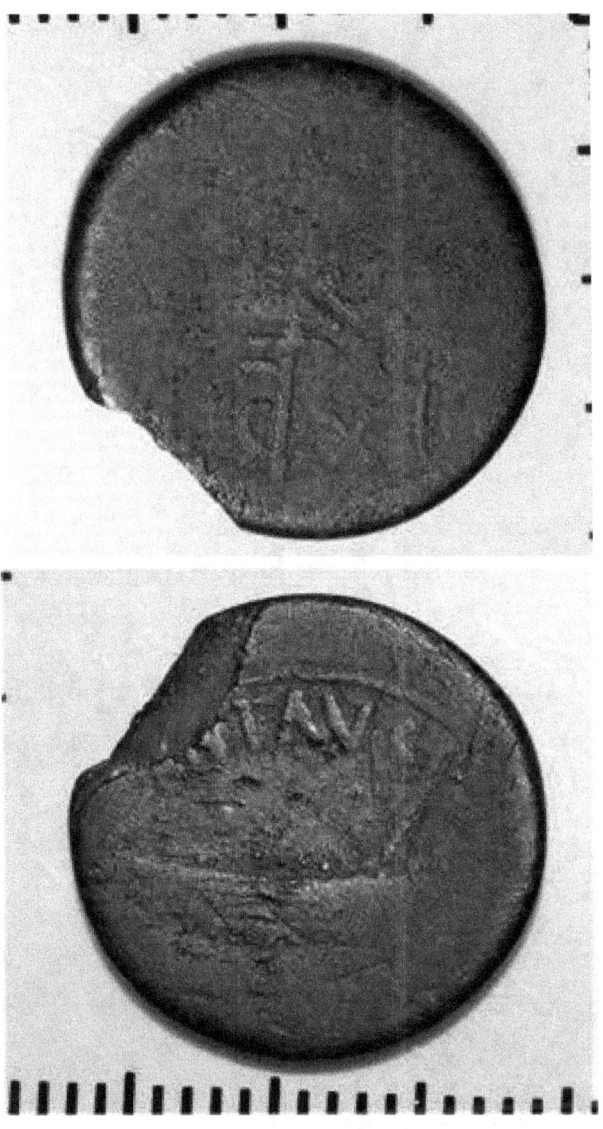

My 29th find is one of my most special but it was on a sad day for us all.

This is a Bronze Age Spear Head which I found in 1997 from 2500 BC.

It was a very hot summer day and the signal was very good and very deep! I dug down in very hard ground about 18 inches before I hit the target and was very careful taking it out.

It came out undamaged just a little potential corrosion but I cleaned it carefully when I got home, as you can see it is in extremely good condition for its age.

I don't think this part of the low-lying field had ever been ploughed and I also think that it used to be flooded and was once part of the River Thet, so my guess is that they were fishing when they lost this spear rather than in battle.

I went home with a big smile on my face until my wife met me at the door and told me Princess Diana had died that morning.

Diana was the Goddess of Hunting to the Romans.

Just Saying!

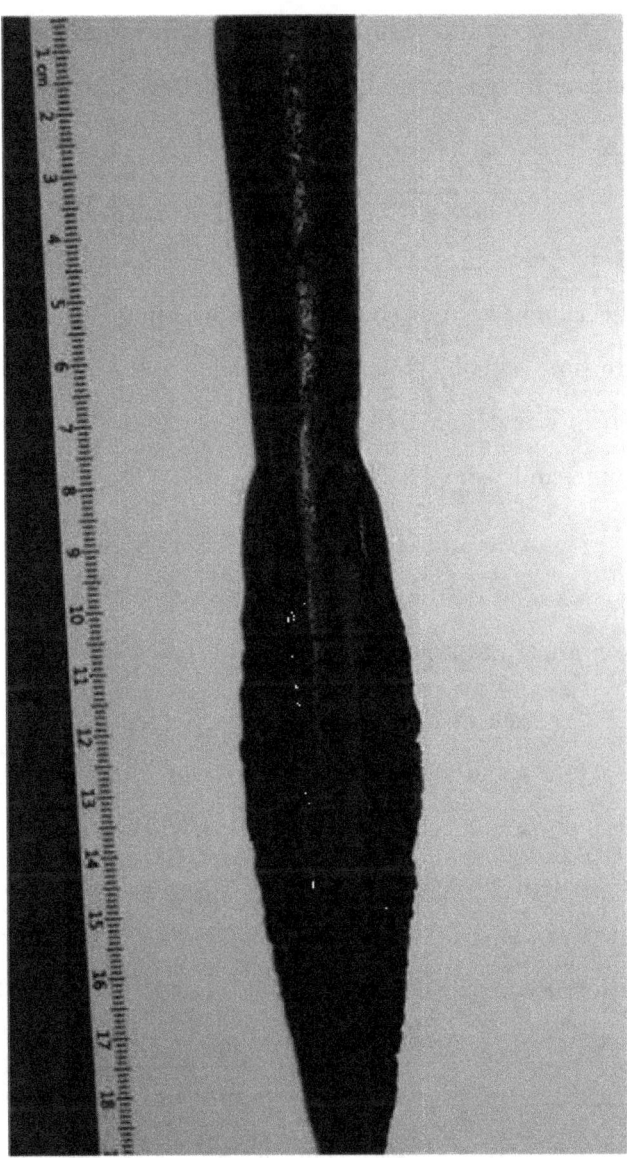

59

My 30th find, I think is linked to a previous special find, although, when I found it I had no idea what it was until I took it to the Castle Museum in Norwich.

This is a Medieval Arm of a Spur which had also been gilded in gold. This would have looked really special when it was complete. My detecting Partner at the time actually found the Rowel at the same time which was designed like a seven-point star with sharp points and also gilded in gold.

The museum suspects that it was a special person like a knight that would have such a nice bit of riding equipment but how did he lose it?

Go back to the finding of the Medieval Knights Gold Ring and we may have the answer. If the Knight in all his gear actually fell off his horse and was dragged along there is a possibility that he not only lost his ring but lost his spur at the same time? My guess at the difference in distance between the items was about 200 yards even though they were found in two different fields, they may well have been in just one at the time. The dates given 14-15th centuries match too and it's a great story for the locals.

61

My 31st find from the '90s is a Medieval Cast Bronze Shield-Shaped Harness Pendant.

Dating from the 13th century it has, according to my helpers in Norwich, a stylised Peacock at the centre with a fanned tail.

They seemed to think it was a Peacock in his pride on the front and on the reverse which I didn't even see, was a label of three points Gules.

This item was drawn at the time by the staff at the Museum as we had no other way to record finds at that time.

Pendants of this type are not very common and some can be collectable and worth a lot of money, like the ones with a coat of arms on, which can be traced to a particular family. If you find one in good condition, you have a rare item.

My 32nd find from the '90s is a Medieval Lead Pilgrim's Ampulla from the 15th century.

These really are a part of our History in the UK and this particular one was from Our Lady of Walsingham Shrine in Norfolk.

The shrine is named after Mary, Mother of Jesus and was venerated by Roman Catholics. Western Rite Orthodox Christians and some Anglicans.

It all started when Lady Richeldis in 1061 AD had apparitions of Mary and so the "Holy House" was built, which became a Shrine and a place of Pilgrimage. A Priory was then built at Walsingham and was passed to the care of the Canons Regular of St Augustine between 1146-1174 AD.

The Shrine was destroyed by Henry VIII in 1538 but restored in 1922 by Father Patten and is still running today.

This ampulla was used to keep holy water from the shrine and would have been hung around the pilgrim's neck.

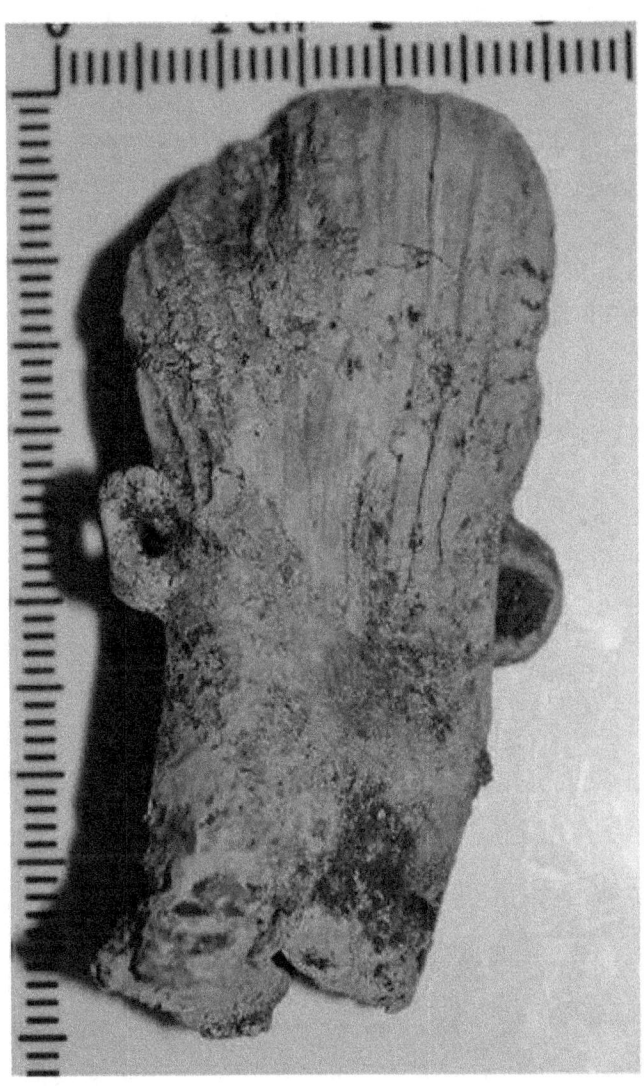

My 33rd find is a really unusual one, and once again I wouldn't expect to find another one!

It is a copper halfpenny token of Shakespeare from North Wales dated 1780.

Obverse: Bust facing left Shakespeare around the head.

Reverse: Crowned Harp with NORTH WALES on either side of the harp.

Like the other tokens, these were minted due to the lack of small change and could be reused to buy other items at a later date.

These were minted in North Wales and given as change, as to the reason Shakespeare was on the obverse side 150 years after he died is a mystery, unless it was because Shakespeare wrote a lot about North Wales in his books and plays?

Who knows?

One thing for sure is that a good one of these would be more valuable than a halfpenny of the same date.

My 34th find is yet another token but this time it is from Norwich.

A copper farthing Dating 1667.

Again these were minted to help the shortage of small change at the time and could be spent later, but the amount of tokens we find, makes you wonder if they bothered and just threw them away?

Obverse: A NORWICH FARTHING 1667.

Reverse: Norwich Town coat of arms consisting of a castle over a lion.

Whilst I was in Norfolk I found quite a few different tokens and I actually found several Norwich ones.

But none are really in excellent condition, they are all fairly well-worn.

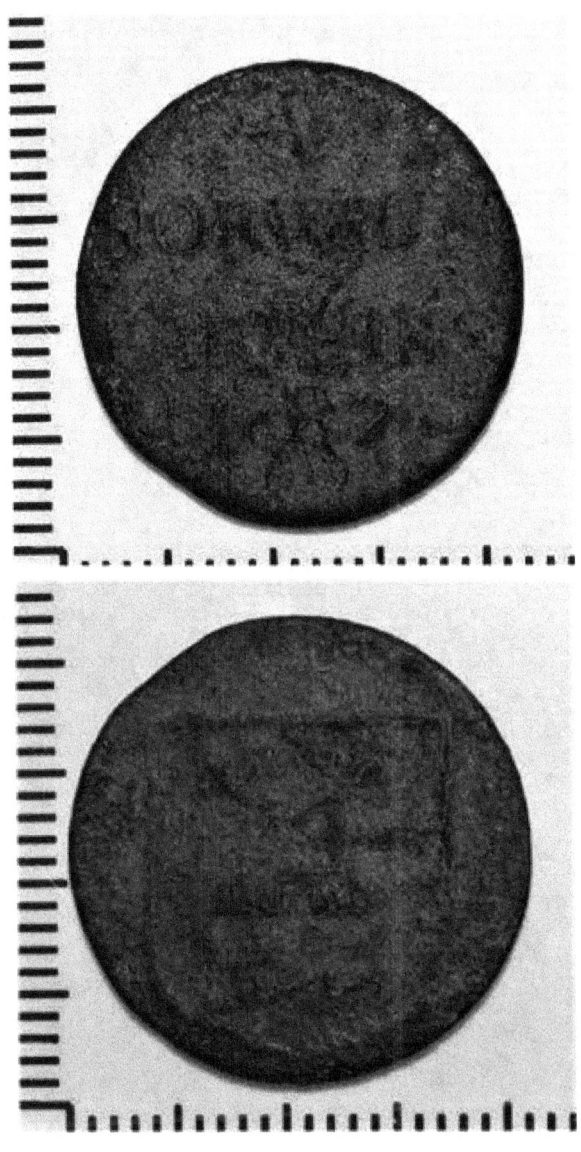

My 35th find from the fields of Norfolk is another token from Norwich.

It is A copper halfpenny token of Norwich dated 1792 and this one is in a lot better condition than the last one, but it is younger!

Obverse: The Arms of Norwich, a triple-towered castle with a gateway, over a lion with a raised paw. "MAY NORWICH FLOURISH" and "PRO BONO PUBLICO" around the castle and lion.

Reverse: The Arms of the Duke of Norfolk, shield with 6 crosses and a diagonal stripe with Lion, over batons, lettering around and date below.

"NORFOLK AND NORWICH HALFPENNY 1792"

Lettering on edge "PAYABLE AT N.BOLINGBROKES HABERDASHER & C. NORWICH.X."

Nathaniel Bolingbroke was a Haberdasher and silversmith with a business in the marketplace in Norwich.

This token is one of my best.

The 36th find from the '90s is another jetton but this time from Germany. Dated 1586-1635 AD these were minted in Nuremberg and one of the most commonest of jetton finds in our soil. This was minted by Hanns Krauwinckel and classed as a Rose Orb type.

Four different members of the same family made these jettons, Damianus, Hans, Egidius and Hanns.

The Rose Orb types apparently account for well over half of the total number of Nuremberg jettons found.

Obverse: Three Crowns, alternately with three lis arranged around a central rose.

Reverse: Imperial Orb within a tressure of three arches and three angles.

These very thin copper alloy tokens always seem to get damaged or come out of the ground falling apart, so to get a good one, you would need to be very lucky!

73

My 37th find in this decade is another rare find in that it is a Personal Seal of a Rich Merchant according to Norwich Castle Museum from the 17-18th centuries.

We have no name but we do know that this bronze seal would have been a part of a ring that swivelled over for him to seal his letters or hung around his neck to achieve the same result.

These seals are very personal and they do not appear from the soil very often. I have 4 in 30 years of detecting and they can be made from all different types of metals.

This type of seal is far more unusual than the chess piece type matrixes that hang around the neck.

People have been using Seals from the Roman times to the present day so there must be few left out there for us to find.

The 38th Item from the '90s is a bronze Roman brooch classed as a Colchester type from 40-65 AD so pretty much when they arrived in Britain.

Roman brooches found in the UK are Common and have lots of different variations in their design and colours used.

But their main task or use, was to hold their robes together and normally came in pairs.

They also come in different sizes from baby size to man size, and unless the owners were highly ranked, the majority of them were bronze.

The most common problem when we find them is that they are either corroding away or broken into bits, but nearly always with no pin like this one.

My 39th find is yet another Roman Brooch but this type, which is also bronze, is classed as a Dolphin Brooch due to the shape and dates from 40-65AD too. So the same period as the former one.

Everything I explained about the last brooch carries over to this one, the only difference is the style of the brooch itself.

Similarly, it was found with no pin!

Very few brooches turned up in my Norfolk fields, so I will show some different ones in the later years.

Some of which are breathtaking...

My 40th find from the '90s is made of solid bronze and was described by the Norwich Castle Museum as a Roman Period toy cauldron!

Once again it is something anyone may not likely find again, but I will say that I did find another had been found on the internet in Holland very similar.

It is solid and would be very heavy as something to keep holy water or something that smells nice in on your person as someone suggested.

It is something that makes you realise that Roman families lived and worked here after they had finished their service, from what I have learned the soldiers each received a slice of land and some money on their retirement.

Over the years I have many items that prove that they very much had a family life here in Britannia, playing, growing up and working in the fields like everyone else, or even better getting someone else to do it!

Some slaves were also able to retire here too.

81

My 41st find from the fields of Norfolk is yet another Roman find, this time it is a solid chunky bronze key handle. This was found less than 10 yards away from the previous item (cauldron).

It was dated to the 1st-2nd century so the person who lost it probably brought it over with them. I have found a few Roman key handles but this was the first and is special, it is also in fairly good condition. Obviously, the iron has corroded away but one would expect that after 2000 years.

There have been many similar Key handles found in the UK, so it does seem to be a common design, but still not a common find.

It is one of those things, you need a lot of luck to find a well-used Roman field, if you manage to find one and gain permission, then you just never know what you will find.

My 42nd find is something I never would have expected to find anywhere! It is a single arm of a pair of Saxon tweezers very kindly identified by Norwich Castle Museum. Dated to the 9th-10th century.

To be honest, I didn't know exactly what it was, but very happy to find it!

It is another item that shows that family life wasn't that much different to our lives today other than we have progressed rather quickly.

Saxon tweezers are not uncommon as one would think judging by the finds.org website and the internet.

They are just normal everyday items today and still, it is surprising to find they have been in use so long.

This, to me, is a special find.

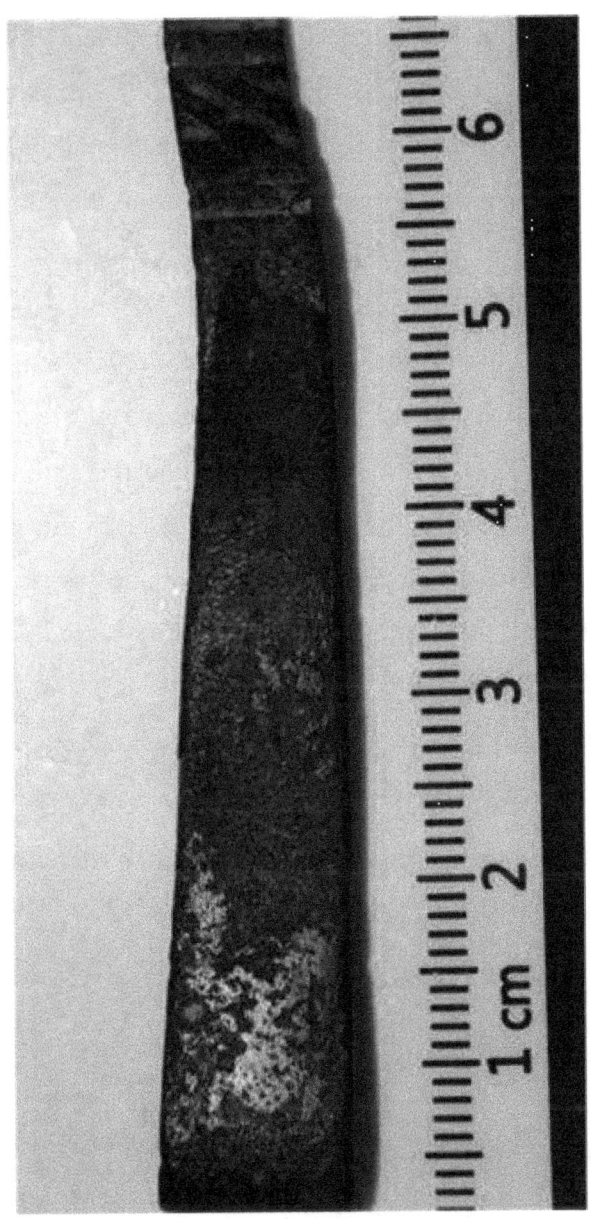

My 43rd find is the first one that I thought was interesting enough to show you that not only metal items can be discovered whilst out walking the fields. This is a Fossil of Sea Urchin from the Upper Cretaceous Period dating back 70-90 Million years. As you would guess it was laid on the surface and not on its own I picked up a couple at the same time, both in really nice condition. Thinking that they had been left by the flood or ice age when I found them, I later found out that Echinoid Fossils were sometimes associated with archaeological sites. The fossils played a part in both Celtic and Norse Mythology, and were venerated, associated with burials, woven into myths and legends and used when making tools and decorative objects.

They are also known as thunderstones, fairy loaves or shepherds' crowns.

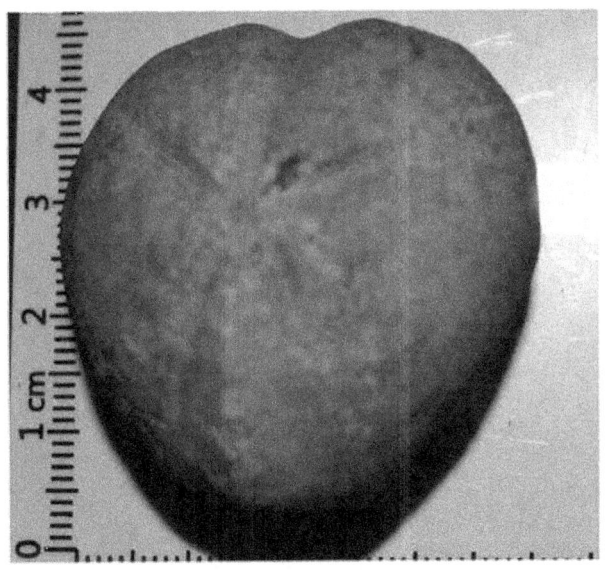

My 44th Item is another item that would have been in daily use in the Post Medieval Period, and this is a silver Bodkin or Headdress Pin.

Dated between 1600 and 1700 this bodkin is slightly bent but that would be expected as silver is quite a soft metal and farm instruments can easily damage them. It seems to be complete otherwise.

Bodkins come in all different metals, so I guess the person who lost this one was a little better off than most.

Today, this would be classed as treasure but when I found this it wasn't required as the law on Treasure trove changed in 1996.

Now any item made from a minimum of 10% silver or gold and is over 300 years old, qualifies as treasure and should be handed to the coroner or your local FLO.

It is another item that was nice to find.

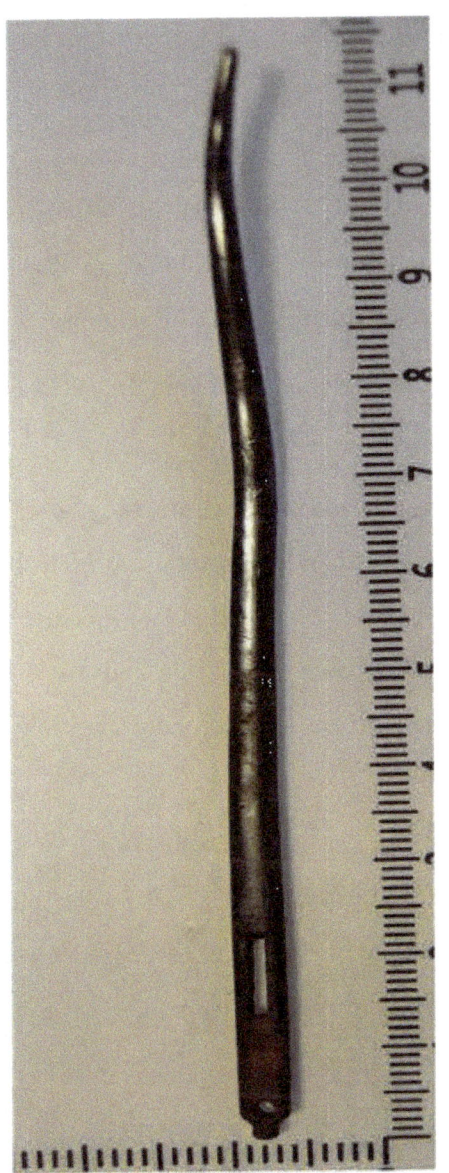

89

My 45th find in the fields of Norfolk came as a big surprise to me!

It is a copper 1-cent coin of Victoria from the Canadian state of New Brunswick. It is dated to 1864 and as this coin was only minted on two occasions 1861 and 1864 that makes it a bit of a rarity in my eyes.

For it to be found in a field in the 1990s in Norfolk beggars belief!

Before Canada became a confederation, some parts issued their own currency and New Brunswick was one of those. A copper Large Cent with a portrait of Queen Victoria on one side and a crown with a wreath with the denomination and date on the other side.

Whoever had this originally, had it punched and probably wore it around their neck as you find through history. They would have been upset to lose it, as it would have been special to them. As it is to me now.

My 46th Item is one of those things you dream of finding a gold coin!

This was the very first gold coin I found and it took nearly 4 years to find it.

It is a gold Half-Sovereign of Victoria dated 1871.

Obverse: Head facing left, VICTORIA DEI GRATIA with date below.

Reverse: Crowned Quartered shield of arms in frame, die number below. BRITANNIARUM REX FID: DEF:

Other than a scratch from the eye downwards it seems in near perfect condition.

It was well worth finding and for those that do, I didn't do the Dance of Gold. I just smiled to myself, happy with my find of the day.

My 47th item is another one-off find and is a silver locket from the Victorian period with a really unusual design. As you can see it has crossed cricket bats with wickets and ball on one side and a floral design with the mint and makers marks on the reverse.

A silver locket, in my mind, is more of a feminine use than a masculine but not to be sexist or anything, I can't get my head around why anyone would have a locket with cricket bats on!

There was no picture inside, by the way, so no clue there then.

It is a special item to someone and as it was different, I included it in this 50.

My 48th item is a lovely silver Half Groat (2 pence) of Henry VII, dated between 1493-5 with a TUN Mintmark which means it was minted in Canterbury. These were issued jointly with Archbishop Morton, facing crowned bust in double tressure of seven arcs, double arched crown, beaded circle and Latin legend surrounding, initial mark tun on both sides. No stops in legend "hEnRIC DI GRA REX AnGLE Z F"

Reverse: long cross pattee, tri pellets in each inner angle, beaded circles and twin concentric legend surrounding, inner legend "CIVI TAS Can TOR", Outer Legend "POSVI DEV A DIVTO E mEV".

This coin looks to be in fairly good condition, although it does look a bit worn or clipped at the edge.

Either way, it is one of my favourites..

My penultimate find from the fields of Norfolk is another copper halfpenny token from 1792. It is classed as a John Harvey's Norwich Weavers Loom halfpenny token.

Obverse: The arms of the City of Norwich consisting of a Lion below a triple-towered castle with the legend "1792".

Reverse: A detailed view of a weaver working on a box loom with a filling wheel on the right.

Edge Inscription "JOHN HARVEY OF NORWICH. XXXX"

John Harvey was the Mayor of Norwich during the year these coins were struck.

I just had to add another local coin before I finished!

My final find from the Norfolk earth is one of my best and rarest. It is pair of copper alloy Anglo Saxon brooches from the 10th century.

According to the Norfolk Museums Service, hundreds of these have been found dotted around East Anglia and nowhere else in the Country.

So I was extremely lucky to find a pair of them in my favourite field.

They show a four-legged animal looking back over their shoulder as it runs.

They date from the early 900s.

Another common find from the Viking Period is Borre-style brooches and what did I find in the very same field?

Yep! A pair of them too! But I am just showing you this pair for now and maybe later I will return with another book of objects from the Norfolk soil.

So to summarise my first 10 Years of detecting, I found 3 gold Items (A Medieval Gold Knights Ring and 2 Half Sovereigns). 3 Roman fields, 1 field that had finds through the ages from Bronze Age to Medieval, and was probably a Market site too. Finally, a field where we know there are the remains of a Celtic Iceni Chariot.

Total Artifacts: 1992 (including buttons and musket balls)

Total coins: 554

I personally don't think I did too bad for a beginner and if you remember when I started, the farmer told me that he had detectorists on his land before, but they never found anything!

Who would you believe?

As a post note I would like to thank all the people based in Norwich Castle Museum who helped in identifying, drawing and dating my finds. (As the National Database was not even started at that time). I would also like to thank my farmer for allowing me to search his fields virtually every week when it was possible.

Finally, I would like to thank my former neighbours Brenda and Francis for getting me into this great hobby in the first place!

The most common finds in our fields are waste products like silver paper which gives an excellent signal; green waste which some farmers allow to be added to their fields along with manure and various mixtures; lead which comes in all guises from the Roman era to present day which really needs to be removed from the field either way as it a nasty substance. We also find iron products which are related to farming through the centuries including horseshoes and plough shards.

Nails and other items too. Cartridge cases are a common find where farmers have been out shooting either pests or for food, but modern-day 12 bore cartridges do not give a signal. Mastitis tubes are also a common find which farmers/workers leave in the field after being used on animals, these also give a great signal, but need digging up and disposal afterwards. There are probably a lot more waste products found but I am just pointing out the most common.

Now for the Common finds we dig up which are a

little more interesting and have a bit of history, buttons, musket and pistol balls, buckles, spindle whorls, badges or brooches, uniform insignia from different periods, medals/medallions, spoons, forks and knives from people which were used to enjoy eating outside in the fields, pottery laid on the surface from all periods from roman to current day, if you keep your eyes open. Toys through the ages, glass shards from the Roman period to today, again laid on the surface. Items from furniture like handles and knobs too. As you can see this is just the start of the items we could find each time we go out with a detector.

The items we would get a buzz from are coins, which have been around for over 2000 years, tokens, jetons, crotal/rumbler bells, Bronze Age items like spearheads, arrowheads, flints from the Neolithic era which you would have to see on the surface, any Iron Age, Roman, Saxon, Viking items and Medieval finds which can be found at any time.

There is always a chance that we can find wartime items like Live or spent ammunition and if you live close to any Army or RAF Bases any kind of any other items like grenades and even mortar bombs and still live Bombs! If you find any of these items you must be very careful if you see them and call the farmer who will call the authorities to deal with them.

Books on all the above subjects are available but are now really expensive to buy so I have tried to give you a little information on some of the items we find.

The Romans and Celts used a button loop fastener which I guess could have been the forerunner for our buttons today. Buttons are virtually found in every field because of the heavy work that the workers would have to do, it would have been easy to wear the thread out and then fall off ready for us to find, some were broken at the top too but one reason that certain fields had more than others goes back to the periods of the Black Death where the clothes of the deceased would be probably burnt in the fields. Many ladies were also working in the fields since we do find quite a few thimbles which we can assume were for repairing or replacing buttons. Thimbles were used in Britain from 1440 AD, these landed in Southampton on a Venetian galley, but they were made in Nurnberg, Germany.

Musket and Pistol Balls These are fairly common finds moulded balls of lead in different sizes. The musket appeared in the 16th century and was capable of piercing plate armour. As time went on the muskets got lighter and eventually turned into rifles as we know them in the 19th century.

Buckles first appeared in Britain by the Romans who used them to fasten the chinstraps of helmet cheek pieces, but they are relatively rare examples, after which they were developed during the Middle Ages to be used on horses saddles, military wear, shoes, belts and straps of all sizes. The older ones seem more decorative and of course, much more sought after.

A Spindle Whorl is a disc or spherical object fitted onto the spindle to increase and maintain the speed of the spin. in the past, they have been made of amber, antler, bone, ceramic, glass, stone, iron, lead and wood. The most common that we find are made of lead and some have nice designs on too.

Badges are something we don't find on a regular basis, but as you know, if we find an old one they are collectable. Badges first appeared in the Middle Ages and were as popular as Jewellery. The Pilgrim badges flourished in the 14th-15th centuries, yet are very rare finds. Heraldic Badges with coat of arms displayed were worn to indicate allegiance to a person or family.

Today we also find Cap and shoulder badges from serving military personnel, and more recently school uniform badges and modern badges which cover absolutely every subject you can think of!

The first recorded brooches were made of thorns and flint, while pins made of metal date back to the Bronze Age. They were not initially worn as jewels but began life like a safety pin, holding pieces of clothing together. Brooches came into their own during the Iron Age and the Roman period where they were made of bronze or silver, and rarely in gold. The design kept getting more lavish through the Saxon, Viking and Medieval periods where their use changed to showing off rather than being a useful item.

Coins are a huge subject which can fill more books than I could ever think of writing about. So I will skim over the subject as there are hundreds of books on the market on every subject.

The first coinage in Britain was made in the Iron Age by the Celts as we know them, each Iron Age tribe had its own boundary the tribe that covered our area of Lincolnshire were the Corieltauvi and the area they called their own was from the Humber Estuary covering all Lincolnshire, Nottinghamshire and most of Leicestershire.

Each Tribe minted their own coinage with different designs on each type of coin, they only used bronze, silver and gold. These coins started appearing in around 150 BC until the Romans arrived in 43 AD.

These coins are not normally found in hoards although some have in other areas of Europe, but we normally find them as single coin finds. This leads experts in the field to suggest that they were donated to their gods for a good harvest or weather.

Roman coinage was uniform in that their coins were the same wherever you went throughout their empire. Gold, silver, brass and bronze.

Gold and silver were issued by the emperor, and brass coins by the senate.

There were three main classes of coinage gold (Aureus) silver (Denarius) and brass (Sestertius, Dupondius and As). Other denominations were also minted but using this formula it is easy to show 2 Asses=1 Dupondius, 2 Dupondii = 1 Sestertius, 4 Sestertius=1 Denarius, 25 Denarius =1 Aureas.

I would love to go through all the emperors and their wives and relatives on their coins but there are thousands, we all need the books to investigate. Unfortunately, most of the Roman coins left in the soil today, do not look like coins at all as the bronze has either crumbled away or worn flat, any silver or gold coins will still be there and hopefully still be complete.

Saxon coins are much harder to find as there are a lot less of them, some Saxons wore Roman coins around their neck, maybe as a trophy or even a gift when the Romans left. The First Saxon coinage was produced by Eadbald of Kent in AD625, these were small gold coins called scillingas (shillings) more recently called thrymsas by numismatists. In the 7th century when gold was harder to come by, they introduced small silver coins known as sceattas minted in England in around 680 AD. These little coins can still be found today, but to date, I haven't found one!

Saxon silver pennies were introduced in the 8th century and later still Gold Solidus and copper stycas were introduced.

Viking coins Rarer still these coins were being minted in Denmark around AD995 Made of silver, they had the name of the ruler and moneyer who minted them. These were then sent to Britain but the invaders used silver bars to trade as well as in pennies.

Medieval coins were normally silver from 1066 AD pennies were introduced under William 1st called short-crossed pennies due to the reverse of the coin having a short cross!

These short cross coins stayed in until 1247 when the Long Cross pennies were introduced under Henry III. These stayed similar until 1547 AD when Edward VI changed the reverse to a shield.

The next change would be under Oliver Cromwell which was the introduction of Milled Coinage in 1656 AD and the end of hammered coins.

Charles II then introduced the first copper coinage in 1672 AD.

Since then the coins have all been milled.

Token coinage was introduced all over the country in the 17th and 18th centuries due to a huge shortage of small change. Which in turn made it difficult to pay workers. So manufacturers and some towns and shops issued their own pennies, half pennies and farthings to pay their workers and give as change so that their customers could go back and spend them another day. These tokens have become very collectable over the years.

Jetons (jettons) were made during the reign of Edward I England 1272-1307 AD, the design of which was similar to the pennies of the time but about the size of a groat and were made of brass. Jetons were also minted in Germany and France and all these types are found in the UK.

Germany soon gained a monopoly over the other countries as they could make them cheaper, but they were much more fragile and very thin. The French jettons were really well made and far better designs and larger than the German Nuremberg jettons.

Jettons were used, not as coinage, as one would presume when you find them but as a counter and used for calculating.

To help you a little with history periods here they are:

- Pre-History ie before Bronze Age
- Palaeolithic: Earliest Stone Age
- Mesolithic
- Neolithic

- Chalcolithic
- Bronze Age
- Iron Age
- Roman Period: 43 - 410 AD
- Saxon Period (Dark Ages) – Early Medieval: 650 - 973 AD
- Late Medieval – Viking Age: 973 - 1066 AD
- Medieval: 1066 - 1450 AD
- Post Medieval: 1450 - 1750 AD
- Modern Era: 1750 AD to Today

Please note that the periods above are not normally split like this as they class the Middle Ages From the 5th century to 1520 AD so this can be confusing. I have tried to help here class the finds better according to the age they come from.

The Romans however have left a huge legacy on our land and we are still finding thousands of items each year that would have been lost if it weren't for us detectorists.

Besides the thousands of coins that are found each year there are all the other signs of Roman habitation for example pottery i.e. Greyware or Samian Ware scattered shards in fields could well mean that a homestead was there.

Brooches (and there are many types) are normally bronze but other far more exotic types have been found but would be classed as treasure and need to be reported.

Other items include spoon handles, key handles, seal boxes and lids, rings, bracelets, dice, knife handles, nail cleaners, ear cleaners, bells, locks, pins, Roman figurines of Gods as well as emperors, mounts of all shapes and sizes from horses and boxes and belts and straps, the list goes on and on.

If they lived in a homestead or a villa, you would have a chance of finding some of these artefacts as well as the coins from around 400 years ago.

I have been very lucky over the years to find some of the above but still get surprised when something different turns up.

The 2000s

In the year 2000, I had to move back to Lincolnshire with my work as a Transport Manager to North Lincolnshire. We moved to just outside Brigg and I was really gutted to leave so much history in the fields of Norfolk. But before I left, I did ask my farmer if he would be kind enough to write me a letter of recommendation which I could show any potential farmers in North Lincolnshire. He did just that and I still have that letter today.

As a total stranger to North Lincolnshire, it was a long time before I could get any permission from anywhere and it seemed a long, slow process. On the other hand, the garden I had inherited in the new house was absolutely massive in comparison to the Norfolk Garden and nearly all my spare time was spent keeping it tidy.

However, eventually after a few years, I did manage to get permission, but not locally to North Lincolnshire; I had to travel a little to detect anywhere.

As it happened, we were moving again 7 years later to just outside Lincoln and things improved greatly. I joined a Metal Detecting Club on the outskirts of

Lincoln, which had a few different farmer's permissions, and I also managed to get a couple of permissions myself.

My Home town is Lincoln, the centre of Lincolnshire, one of the country's top 3 areas for treasure finds and a huge amount of history in and around it.

I just couldn't wait to get out into the fields around us. I did purchase a White's Spectrum within this time period and found more smaller items with it.

I would like to point out that most of my finds during this period and the 2010s were identified by our local FLO and photographed by them too.

The descriptions are mostly taken from the Nationwide Database as they have been written by the FLO's, with their permission, along with a few photos too.

The following finds are in no particular order or value, some of them are damaged in antiquity and are included to show the damage caused over the years in the soil.

I hope you enjoy the selection over this 10-year period and I must apologise for some of the photography, which may seem a little blurred, probably too much wine celebrating my finds! But I promise you, I am improving.

One of my first finds from the soil of Lincolnshire were an eyes-only find; as I was walking around a field not far from Bardney, I came across all these ammonites just sitting on the surface. I have no doubt at all that there would be more underneath but we didn't have such a thing as an excavator at the club on that day!

Ammonites lived during the periods of Earth's history known as the Jurassic and Cretaceous periods. Together, they represent a time period of 140 million years. The Jurassic Period began about 201 million years ago and the Cretaceous Period ended 66 million years ago. The ammonites became extinct at the end of the Cretaceous, at roughly the same time as the dinosaurs disappeared. However, a lot is known about them because they are commonly found as fossils formed when the remains or traces of the animal became buried by sediments that later solidified into rock.

Where Lincoln stands today is a part of the tract of Jurassic rocks which cover an area from the Humber Estuary down to Southampton.

As I have mentioned before, in the '90s, it pays to keep your eyes open; no man has ever touched these before I did! It is a really weird feeling!

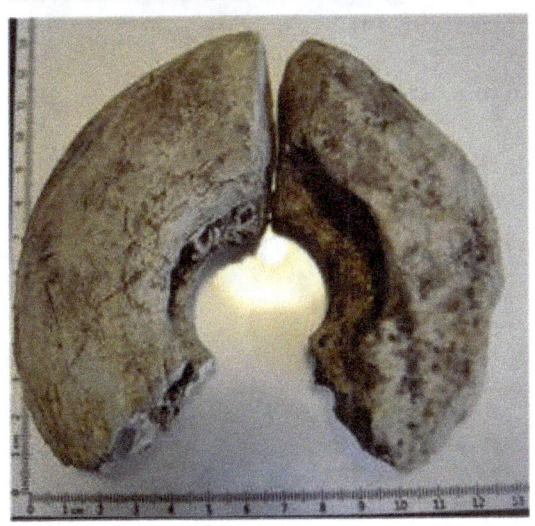

My 2nd find From Lincolnshire is a copper alloy Crotal Bell which, when cleaned, still rang nice and clear.

It is in a reasonable condition no damage anywhere, which is unusual, and this makes it special.

Crotal Bells were first made in Europe before the Middle Ages and though many founders cast bells of this type, the Robert Wells bell foundry of Aldbourne, Wiltshire, produced the largest range.

The first designs came in 2 halves into which a metal pea was added and then they were soldered together. Around 1400 AD, they were cast in one single piece with a ball of metal inside.

They were used on horse-drawn vehicles and other animals like cattle, goats and sheep. They are a really nice thing to find and getting more difficult to get a complete one.

What is the worst possible thing you can imagine digging up whilst metal detecting? In my eyes, we expect a large amount of rubbish in the fields, lead, iron, green waste and lots of silver paper, but it is to dig up a lovely rare find that is broken!

In this case a beautiful Roman silver Denarius of Caracalla.

This coin was minted with Antoninvs Pivs AVG around a young head.

Reverse shows Caracalla, naked, standing, facing, holding globe and resting on a spear. Around it is RECTOR ORBIS. It was minted in Rome in 201 AD.

He was the emperor from 198-217 AD and was formerly Marcus Aurelius Antoninus, He ruled alongside his father, Septimius Severus and later with his brother Geta, who was murdered and it was suspected on the orders of Caracalla.

Caracalla himself, was also assassinated by a disaffected soldier in 217 AD. It is a real shame about the damage to the coin though!

My 4th item is one that is not found too often I understand. It is a coin weight from Charles I, dating from 1625-1640.

This was Identified by the local FLO at the time in Lincoln. Yet no one has actually let me know for which coin it was for!

It is made of bronze, and has the royal crown but there are no numerals on the face to compare with coins of the time. We do know it had to be either a gold or a silver coin, because that was all they used to make the coins at that time.

The reverse is not in good condition and had a touch of bronze disease, which effectively erases anything that was there in the first place.

Nevertheless, it is a part of our history. And I was the lucky person to pick it up this time!

My 5th item from the soil of Lincolnshire is a copper alloy Dupondius of Claudius I, dated 41-54 AD. So, really from the date the Romans invaded our shores. This particular coin was identified by Scunthorpe Museum FLO.

It is not in the best of conditions, it has bronze disease in places, and that takes its toll on a coin.

Obverse: TI CLAVDIVS CAESAR AVG PM TR IMP Bare Head Left

Reverse: SC across Field, Minerva standing Right Brandishing spear and holding a shield.

His full name was Tiberius Claudius Caesar Augustus Germanicus; he was the first Roman emperor to be born outside Italy, in Lugdunum Gaul. (Lyon) Mark Antony was his maternal grandfather. He had four wives and at least six children one of which was Nero, who was adopted.

He passed away in 54 AD, aged 63—not bad for a Roman!

My 6th find in Lincolnshire probably doesn't look much, but this is what the majority of bronze Roman coins look like when you pull them out of the ground after 2000 years, or worse!

This one, identified by our Lincoln FLO, is a bronze radiate of Claudius II, dated 268-70 AD.

A barbarous radiate is an imitation of the antoninianus, a type of coin issued during the Roman Empire, which is named due to its crude style and prominent radiate crown worn by the emperor. These radiates were issued privately during the crisis of the 3rd century in the western provinces, and are not generally regarded as forgeries. They were probably regarded as small change.

Marcus Aurelius Claudius Gothicus was known as Claudius II, who was emperor from AD268-70 when he was overcome by the Plague of Cyprian that had ravaged the provinces of the Roman Empire.

Up to 95% of Roman bronze coins are like this or worse when recovered.

My 7th find of the 2000s is another copper alloy Roman coin. This time, a Sestertius of Commodus dating to 186 AD. Sestertii are the largest and chunkiest of Roman coins, most seem to come out of the soil very well-worn or damaged. But at least we can see enough of this one to ID and date it!

A Sestertius was valued at 100th of a Gold Aureus until the late 3rd century when it ceased being minted.

Commodus was a Roman Emperor who served jointly with his father, Marcus Aurelius, from 176 AD until his father died in 180 AD, and then solely until 192 AD. His reign is commonly thought of as marking the end of a golden period of peace in the history of the Roman Empire, known as Pax Romana. He was made the youngest consul in Roman history in 177 AD. However, he was assassinated in 192 AD by a wrestler in the bath!

This particular coin has bronze disease in places and if it hadn't been dug up, it would be in a real sorry state now!

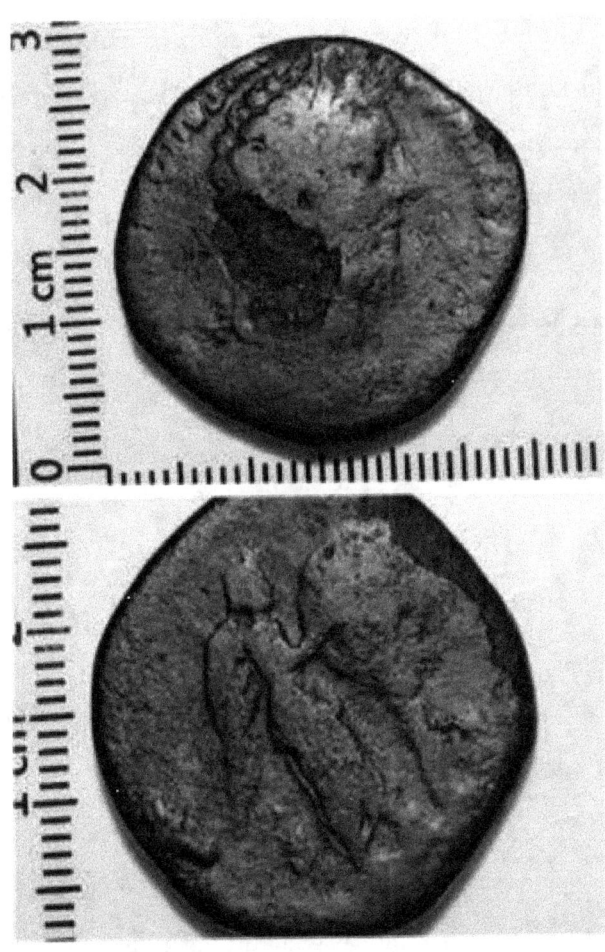

My 8th find from Lincolnshire is a nummus of Constantine I, dated 330-6 AD by Scunthorpe Museum. It is not in the best of condition once again, but people need to actually see and understand that not all finds come out of the ground in perfect condition.

The term 'nummus' means a low-value coin and, therefore can include a swathe of low-value Roman coins, and seems to be an easy way to describe these coins. It is classed as a late Roman coin made of copper alloy.

Constantine the Great reigned from 306-337 AD, and he began the transition of Christianity to be the dominant religion of the Roman Empire, which could have been brought about by the influence of his mother, Helena, who was a Christian.

His decision to cease the persecution of Christians in the Roman Empire was a turning point for early Christianity, and ultimately brought about the decriminalising of Christian worship.

Although this coin doesn't look the best, believe me when I say 90% or more of Roman bronze coins come out of the soil a lot worse than this.

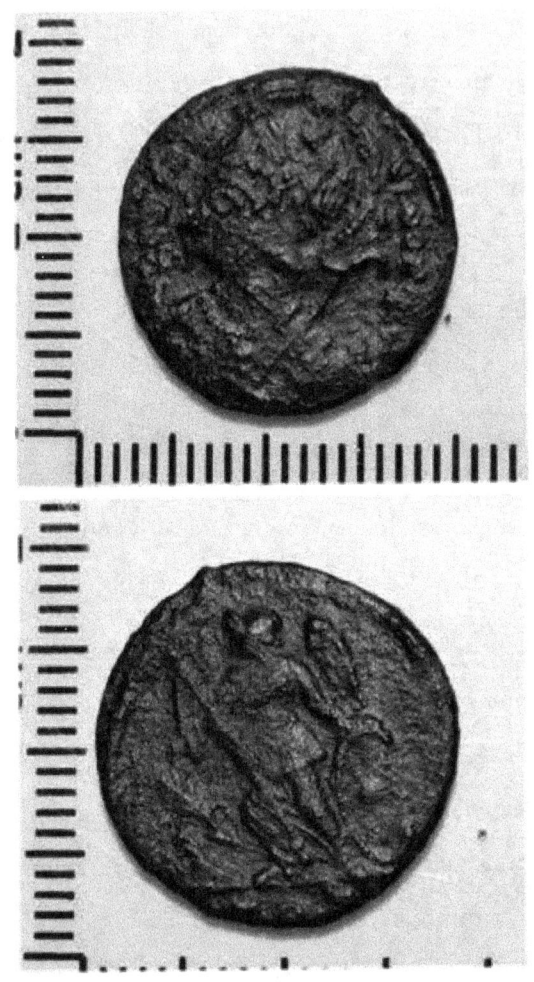

My 9th item from the soils of Lincolnshire is another bronze nummus of Constantine I dated to 318-24 AD. This bronze coin is in far better condition than the last one as you can see, and very few come up in this condition and better.

Constantine I, whose full name was Flavius Valerius Constantinus, was known as Constantine the Great. He was born in Naissus, Dacia Mediterranea, now Serbia. He was the son of Flavius Constantius and his mother was Helena, who was Greek and apparently of low birth, but appeared on some of his coins.

He fought alongside his father in Britain and after his father's death in 306 AD, he became emperor and acclaimed by his army at Eboracum (York). He emerged victorious in the civil wars against emperors Maxentius and Licinius to become the sole ruler of the Roman Empire in 324 AD.

My 10th find from the noughties is yet another bronze nummus of Constantine I and dated to 335 AD precisely by our FLO in Lincoln.

The obverse shows the helmeted bust of Roma facing left with VRBS ROMA written around it. The reverse shows a wolf suckling twins, with stars over. It comes from the Mint of Rome.

This is the coin that tells the story of the birth of Rome in mythology, Romulus and Remus, the twin brothers, whose story tells the events that led to the founding of Rome by Romulus. The killing of Remus by his brother has inspired artists through the years. Since ancient times, the image of the she-wolf suckling the twins has been a symbol of the city of Rome. The story itself takes place in 750 BC so well before Rome was built. The twins were born in Alba Longa, an ancient Latin City near where Rome is now situated.

To find a coin with this picture on is special, because we all know the story!

My 11th find from the noughties is a copper alloy buckle dated to Post-Medieval era, so it covers a few hundred years, and was found just outside Lincoln. I had to include at least one buckle as they are a common find but very rarely complete due to rusting away of vital parts and plough damage.

This is a tiny shoe buckle which would have been silvered originally, dated between 1600-1800 AD.

Buckles, as today, came in lots of different shapes and sizes for belts, shoes and straps from humans as well as animals.

They have been in use since the Roman times therefore 2000 years of use, so there should be a lot still in the ground for people to find, even silver ones!

My 12th find of this 10-year period is one of the tiniest coins one would hope to find. It is a silver farthing from Edward I dated 1272-1307 and minted in London. For the age, it is in really nice condition and not as damaged as a lot would be, due to the size.

Obverse: Crowned Head Facing, EDWARDVS REX Around

Reverse: CIVITAS LONDON.

There were a few different mints used for these; besides London, there were Berwick, Bristol, Lincoln, Newcastle and York.

Little is known of medieval farthings, for only a few examples remain today. As the smallest denomination, it was rarely hoarded and has never been found in large hoards. They only contained a quarter of the silver of a penny, meaning they are extremely small, and therefore easily lost, which is why only a few of today's metal detectors can find them. They were not produced in large quantities, like the pennies, though they were useful for small purchases, as a consequence they are rare today.

My 13th find from the noughties is the remains of a Hammered silver penny from Edward III. It may be in a shocking state, but it is very common to find them badly damaged.

The report from our FLO is as follows:

A medieval silver penny of Edward III. Mint of Reading. Class 15d. First coinage struck 1327-43.

Obverse description: Crowned bust facing

Obverse inscription: ()NGL'DNS()

Reverse description: Long Cross, three pellets in three angles, scallop shell in one angle.

Reverse inscription: VILL(AR ADI)NGY

I was informed when I collected it from the FLO that it was a rare find in Lincolnshire, so rare it was the first ever found in our county from this particular mint.

That is the reason I selected this particular coin even though it is badly damaged.

The 14th find of this decade is another Medieval silver penny, this time of Edward IV (1471-83 AD). The Actual date of the coin is 1476-80 AD, and struck at the York Mint under Archbishop Lawrence Booth.

The FLO report continues:

Obverse description: Crowned Bust Facing, B to left and key to right of bust.

Obverse inscription: Illegible

Reverse description: Long Cross, three pellets in angles, quatrefoil in the centre.

Reverse inscription: CIVITAS EBORACI

Edward IV was King of England from 1461 to 1470, then again from 1471 to 1483. He was a central figure in the War of the Roses, a series of civil wars in England fought between the Yorkist and Lancastrian factions between 1455 and 1487. Edward was born in Rouen, France, in 1442; he Married Elizabeth Woodville and they had eight children together. Edward died in 1483 and is buried in St George's Chapel.

This coin is pretty well-worn, but from an unusual mint for me, this is why I included it.

147

My 15th item is a lovely silver sixpence of Elizabeth I, dated 1578 AD, minted in London.

The report says:

Obverse description: Crowned bust left with rose behind head.

Obverse inscription: ELIZABETH.D. G. ANG FR ET HI REGINA

Reverse description: Long Cross fourchee over royal shield with date above shield.

Reverse inscription: POSVI DEV. AD/IVTORE/M.MEV

Initial Mark Plain Cross

Elizabeth's coins are notorious for having a badly minted obverse side and therefore they look worn. Elizabeth was the daughter of Henry VIII and Anne Boleyn, born in 1533 AD and was referred to as the Virgin Queen. Her mother was executed when she was only 2 years 6 months old. Elizabeth was crowned as the Queen in 1559 AD and ruled until 1603, when she passed away in Richmond Place, Surrey. Her coffin was carried downriver at night to Whitehall on a barge lit with torches, and she was laid to rest in Westminster Abbey.

149

My 16th item of this decade is a silver sixpence of George III, dated 1819.

Obverse description: Laureated Bull Head facing Right.

Obverse inscription: GEOR:III D:G BRITT:REX F:D 1816

Reverse description: Crowned shield in Centre with 2 rings circling one within the other.

Reverse inscription: HONI SOIT O MAL Y PENSE

These George III sixpences with the bull head are really nice to find.

George was born in 1738 AD at Norfolk House in St James Square, London. He was the Grandson of George II, and eldest son of Frederick, Prince of Wales.

He Married Charlotte of Mecklenberg-Strelitz and had 15 children. He ascended to the throne at the age of 22 on the death of George II.

In later years, he suffered not only with mental problems, but was also virtually blinded by cataracts and in pain with rheumatism. In 1811, he became permanently insane and lived in seclusion at Windsor Castle until he died in 1820. He was buried in Windsor Castle.

My 17th find of the decade is a Roman silver siliqua of Gratian dating to 378-83 AD, minted in Trier.

The report on the National Database says:

A Late Roman silver siliqua of Gratian.

Obverse description: Pearl diademed, draped and cuirassed bust right.

Obverse inscription: DN GRATIA-NVS PF AVG

Reverse description: Roma seated left on cuirass, holding victory on globe and reversed spear.

Reverse inscription: VRBS ROMA

Mintmark: TRPS

Flavius Gratianus was emperor of the western part of the empire from 367 to 383 AD. Born 359 AD, he was the eldest son of Valentinian I, and was only 8 years old when he became emperor. He married twice due to his first wife, Flavia Maxima Constantia, passing away at the age of 21. Gratian himself was killed in Lugdunum (Lyon) in 383 AD, and is buried in Milan.

My 18th find is another Roman silver coin, this time a Denarius of Hadrian dated to 123 AD.

The FLO Report is as follows:

A silver Denarius of Hadrian

Obverse description: Laureate head right.

Obverse inscription: IMP CAESAR TRAIAN HADRIANUS (AVG)

Reverse description: Aequitas standing left, holding scales and cornucopia.

Reverse inscription: PM TR P COS III

Born Publius Aelius Hadrianus, he was adopted by Trajan and took over from Trajan as emperor when he passed away.

Hadrian reigned from 118-138 AD (20 years). He married Trajan's grand-niece Vibia Sabina, and they adopted 2 children, Ludius Aelius Caesar and Antoninus Pius.

Hadrian passed away in 138 AD in Baiae, Italy and is buried in Hadrian's Mausoleum. This is a lovely coin in really nice condition too. I am very lucky to have found it.

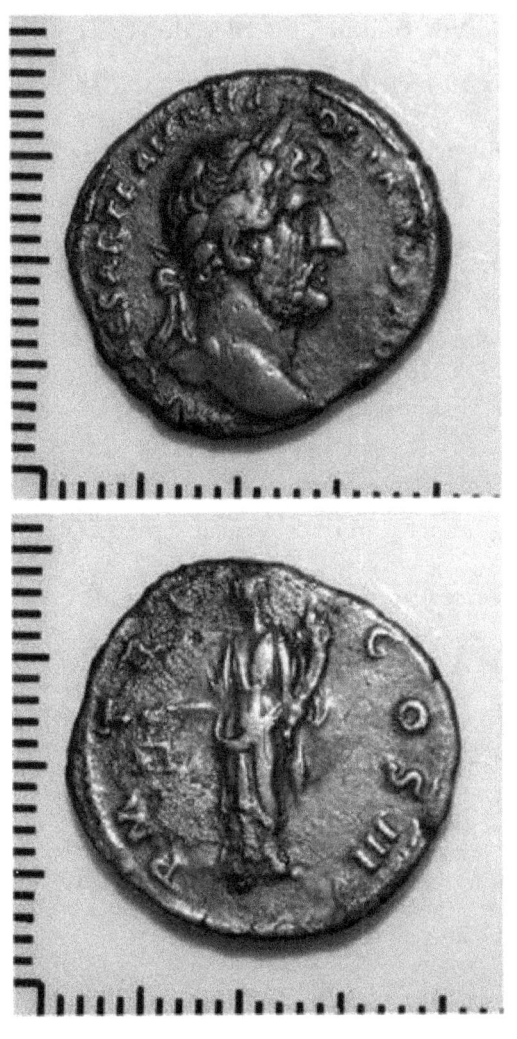

155

My 19th offering this decade is a copper alloy nummus of Helena dating to 337-40 AD.

Identified by Scunthorpe FLO, the report as follows:

A worn copper alloy Roman nummus of Helena

Obverse description: Draped bust right

Obverse inscription: F L IVL HE-LENA AVG

Reverse description: Pax standing facing left holding branch and transverse sceptre.

Reverse inscription: PAX PV-BLICA

Helena was the first wife of Constantius I and mother of Constantine I. She was abandoned by her husband but brought to the Imperial court by her son and given many titles. Famed for her piety, Helena is a saint in the Eastern Orthodox, Oriental Orthodox and Roman Catholic churches.

Flavia Julia Helena was born between 246-8 AD. She married Constantius Chlorus. She died in 330 AD, and is buried in the Mausoleum of Helena.

My 20th item is a silver Half Groat of James I dated to 1618 AD besides a bend in the coin due to plough damage, it is in fairly good condition. The report is documented as:

Obverse description: At the centre within a circle of beads, a rose: above, crown: around I D G ROSA SINE SPINA

Reverse description: At the centre within a circle of beads, a thistle: above, crown: around TVEATVR UNITA DEVS

London Mint.

James was the son of Mary, Queen of Scots, and a great, great grandson of Henry VII, King of England and Lord of Ireland and therefore a potential successor to all three thrones. He was only 13 months old when he ascended the Scottish throne, after his mother was forced to abdicate.

He reigned from 1603-1627 AD.

He married Anne of Denmark and had seven children. He died in 1625 aged 58 in Hertfordshire and is buried in Westminster Abbey.

This is one of the few coins made that doesn't show the head of the king or queen.

159

My 21st find is a cut silver halfpenny of either King John or Henry III, there was some doubt about this with the FLO in Lincoln. The report reads:

A silver cut halfpenny, probably of John or Henry III, moneyer Walter but mint uncertain struck 1199-1247 AD.

Obverse description: Crowned Bust facing, sceptre in right hand.

Obverse inscription: ()ENRI()

Reverse description: Voided Short cross, quatrefoil in angles.

Reverse inscription: WALTE()

The coin itself is in really nice condition and these cut half pennies are a nice find. Some are more common types than others, the early ones like this one are not so common. Although Edward I are very common.

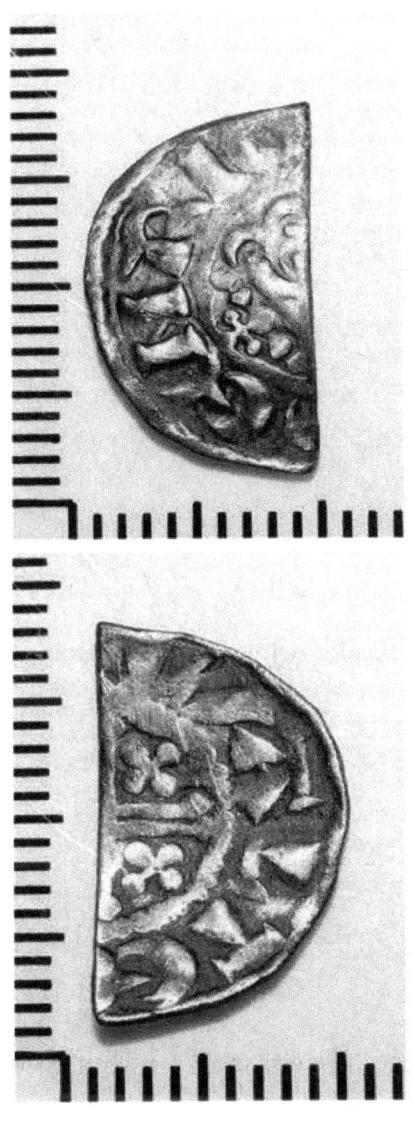

161

My 22nd find of this decade is yet another Roman silver siliqua, this time it is of Julian II dated 361-3 AD and minted in Lyon.

The report on the database is as follows:

Obverse description: Rosette diademed, draped and cuirassed bust right.

Obverse inscription: FL CL IVLIA-NVS PP AVG

Reverse description: VOTIS/V/MVLTIS/X in Wreath

Reverse inscription: VOTIS/V/MVLTIS/X

Flavius Claudius Julianus was a Roman Emperor from 361-3 AD as well as a notable philosopher and author in Greek. He was born in Constantinople in 331 AD, and married Helena in 355 AD.

Julian was mortally wounded in the battle of Samarra in 363 AD and was succeeded as Emperor by Jovian.

Julian died in Frygium, Mesopotamia and was buried in Tarsus.

A strange note on these siliqua coins is that most I find have a crack in them as though it was done on purpose. But other than that, this one is ok!

My 23rd find is a copper alloy post-medieval clothes/dress hook.

The report from the database is short and sweet:

A post-medieval copper alloy dress hook. The body is circular, domed, and decorated around the perimeter with pellets. The central boss appears to contain a rose motif. The loop is trapezoid and the hook is intact.

Dated between 1500-1600 AD.

Clothes Hooks are not uncommon finds to us detectorists, but finding an undamaged one is a lot rarer.

The picture below right shows how these hooks were worn to hold the ladies' dresses up to keep them from getting dirty and wet.

165

My 24th find of this decade is a Rare Saxon copper alloy Stirrup Mount dating from 1025-1100 AD.

The Database report is as follows:

A Late Saxon copper alloy openwork mount. Only the upper half survives. The apex is in the form of a trefoil, and contains a copper alloy rivet. The body is openwork and the frame on either side is possibly formed by a beast, defined by incised lines. The lower half is missing. The object has a reddish patina.

The mount has some resemblance to stirrup strap mounts of Williams Class A, so it is probably along those lines.

Any items from the Saxon/Viking Periods are not common at all and are always nice if you can find anything, even if it is a 'part-efact'.

The advent of metal detectors has, however, brought a large increase in Saxon finds and helped the FLOs build up a much better picture of their whereabouts over the last few years.

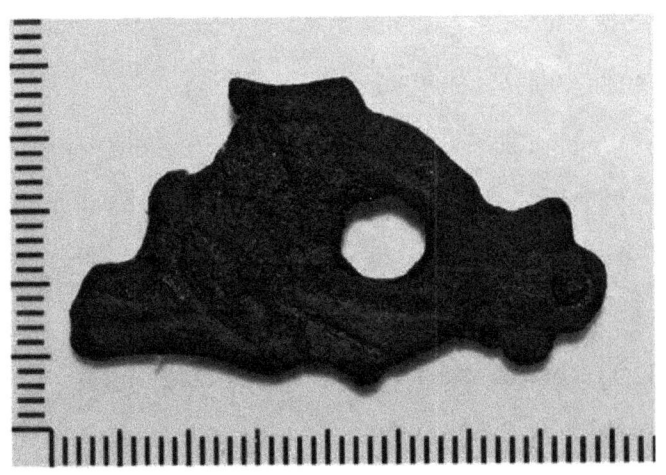

My 25th find of the decade is a Medieval copper alloy Horse Harness Pendant dating to 1200-1400 AD.

The report from the database says:

The pendant is shield-shaped and has an integral loop at the top. The shield is decorated with a lion passant left in the top field; the area below is hatched with reserve metal. The recessed fields would once have contained enamel.

Such a shame that all the enamel is now gone; it would truly have been a lovely find, not that it isn't now!

These Heraldic pendants are not very common and I have been lucky to find three different ones in 30 years.

My 26th find in this section is A copper alloy five-centime piece of Napolean III, dated 1863, and in immaculate condition too.

Obverse description: Bust with goatee left. Mint Marked anchor to the left and cross to the right of the date.

Obverse inscription: NAPOLEAN III EMPEREUR 1863

Reverse description: Imperial spread eagle with mintmark of overlapping BB Below.

Reverse inscription: EMPIRE FRANCAIS CINQ CENTIMES.

These copper coins are not uncommon in the fields of the UK, but most are in worse condition than this one.

Charles-Louis Napolean Bonaparte was born in Paris in 1808. He married Eugenie de Montijo in 1853. They had 3 children.

Because of a failed coup against King Louis-Phillipe, he ended up in England. He died in Chislehurst in 1873 and was buried in Farnborough.

My 27th find is extra special to me. It is a Neolithic Flint Axe Head found near Bardney.

The FLO report is as follows:

A Neolithic polished flint axe. The axe is incomplete, with perhaps approximately just over half of the original length remaining. The axe is rectangular in plan with a curved cutting edge. In cross-section, the axe is pointed oval. The flint is mottled light brown in cross-section with various chalky-coloured fault lines running through it. On the surface, the axe has a mottled reddish-brown appearance.

It has been dated to between 4000-2000 BC.

Detectorists rely on the signals they get from their machines to pinpoint their finds, it really helps to keep your eyes open too, because one could literally walk over something like this and miss a very special piece of history. I have found some amazing things over the 30 years which have been eyes only, and this is one of them, on a foggy day too!

173

My 28th find is a copper alloy Nuremberg Jetton of Hanns Krauwinckel II

Dated to 1561-1650 AD

The report on the database is as follows:

Obverse description: Three crowns and three lis around a central rose.

Obverse inscription: HANNS KRAVWINCKEL IN NVR

Reverse description: Reichsapfel

Reverse inscription: GOT () SOL MAN LOB

These jettons are so very thin that most of them come out of the soil either broken or incomplete or very worn. It is very unusual to find one undamaged, so very pleased with this one.

Jettons are an alternative to currency and were produced to perform calculations for accountancy. Nuremberg jettons are the most common types found in our fields, and the English ones are much rarer.

My 29th find of this decade is yet another one off as I am very unlikely to find another one of these! It is a Papal Bullae (Seal) of Pope Gregory IX dating to 1227 AD.

The PAS Database report says:

Approximately half of a lead papal bulla, probably of Pope Gregory IX. The right half remains, which displays the bust of St Peter within a beaded border. The bust of St Paul would originally have decorated the left side of the obverse. Above the bust is the inscription (SPAS)PE, abbreviations for St Paul and St Peter. The reverse has the inscription of the pope (GRE)/GOR (IUS)/PP VII(II). PP is an abbreviation for pastor pastorum, which translates as "shepherd of the shepherds". The bulla appears to have been cut in half along the line of the central hole through which a chord would have originally been threaded.

Papal bullae were used as seals on official papal documents to authenticate their provenance and authority and were often reused as religious amulets.

Dated between 1227-1241 AD.

So basically, I could have been the second person to hold this seal, following the person to whom it was sent by the pope! Amazing bit of history.

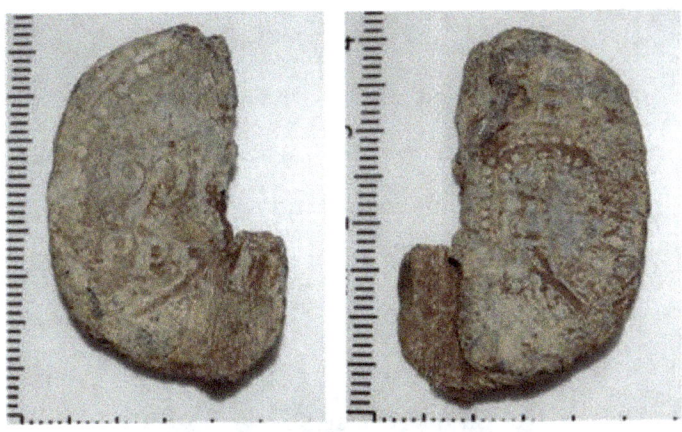

My 30th find of this decade is a Roman bronze bow and fantail brooch dating to between 75-150 AD.

The Database report says:

An incomplete early Roman copper alloy bow and fantail brooch. Only the foot survives. The foot is triangular and contains three pointed oval motifs in reserve metal; each pointed oval has a recessed circular cell in its centre; blue enamel survives in two cells. This motif appears to be a variant of the more commonly seen hanging pelta motif. The background is also recessed and contains traces of red enamel. A catch plate survives on the reverse.

The metalwork of the Romans was amazing and to think this and thousands of other artefacts like it come up after 2000 years and still you can see the colours on some of them. It would have looked lovely and shiny when worn at the time.

It would be great to know who actually was the one to wear it!

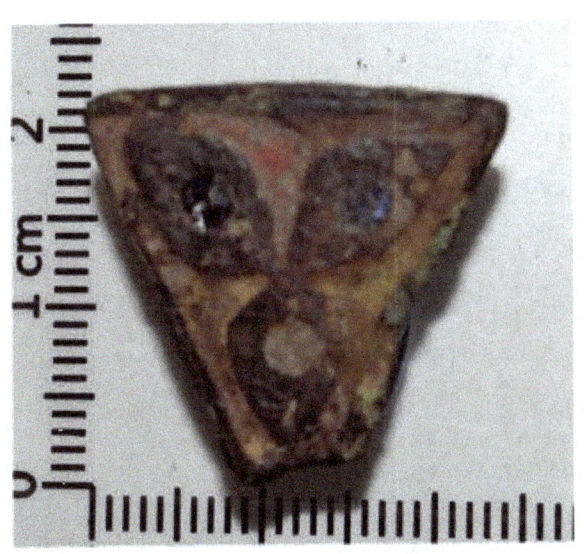

179

My 31st item is also Roman and made of bronze, this is another item that was returned back to me without being logged onto the database for some reason.

However, I have been fortunate enough to find four Roman bells over the past few years and they do have a similar one to this on the database and found only a few yards away from this one!

The database states that it is a Roman copper alloy bell with a Lozenge shaped suspension loop. The body of the bell has a tiny piece missing but otherwise virtually complete and is circular in shape around the base. The clapper is missing in this instance but the remaining bell is in remarkable condition.

Dating between 43-410 AD.

Romans often used bells on their tintinnabulas but I won't go into that one any further!

My 32nd find of this decade is a Roman Crossbow Brooch dating to 290-350 AD.

The report on the PAS Database is as follows:

An incomplete later Roman copper alloy Crossbow Brooch. The wings are octagonal in section and both terminate with a solid bulbous head. The bow is triangular in section. An integral bulbous head extends at the top, and this is sat on a collar. A slot for a hinged pin is located in the centre on the reverse of the wings.

The brooch appears to be unfinished; additional copper alloy is seen forming a triangular plate between the faces of the wings and the bow on both sides. One would expect these plates to have been trimmed off during the finishing process.

This type of brooch was made particularly for the Roman soldiers, So the deduction seems to be that the Romans were actually making these brooches on the site I have found!

Well that's impressive!

My 33rd item of the noughties is another Roman brooch, this time a Dolphin Brooch. The report is as follows:

An incomplete hinged dolphin brooch dating to the early Roman Period. The wings are undecorated and are cylindrical in cross-section, containing an axis bar for a hinged pin. The pin is missing. The bow is oval in cross-section, undecorated and comma-shaped in profile. The foot and catch plate are missing.

Dated 75-150 AD.

The size of this brooch leads me to think it is a child's brooch, which also points to families being in the vicinity too. When we think of the Romans, we do not normally think of them having a family life here, but they did and the evidence is there for us all to see.

I also found a matching brooch later on, so I have now found a matching pair of tiny child's brooches.

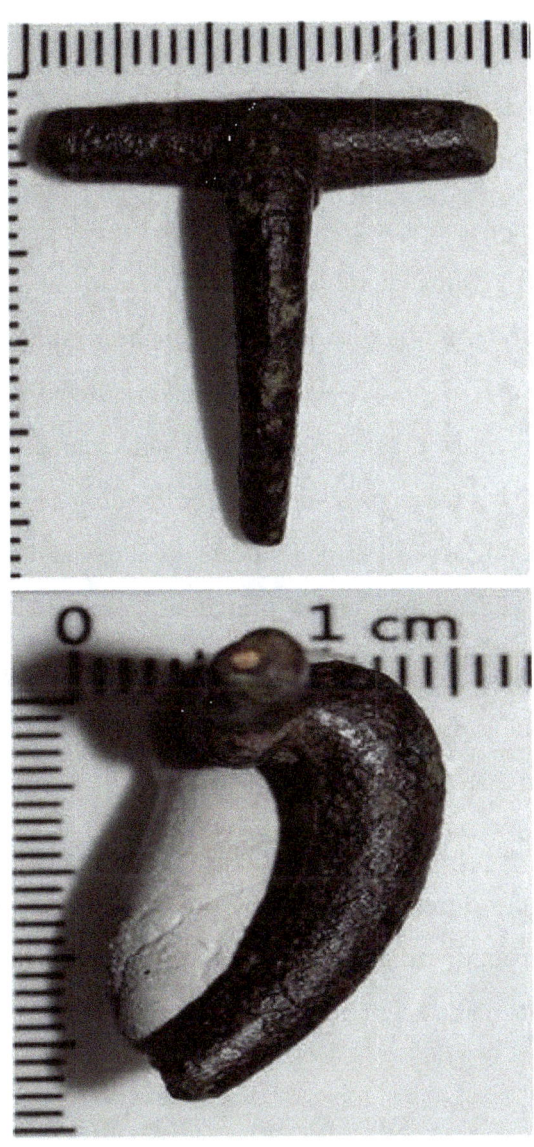

My 34th item of the decade is a Roman Fish Brooch Dated to 75-150 AD.

The FLO report on the database is as follows:

An incomplete zoomorphic plate brooch dating to the early Roman period. The brooch is made of copper alloy and is in the form of a fish. The head and tail are missing. The body is flat, oval and decorated with a deep perimeter that was once filled with enamel. In the middle is a raised panel decorated with incised grooves mimicking scales. A small fin extends above and below at the tail end. A spring is located on the reverse.

Roman brooches were made in all different ways, this one is my most unusual in the shape of a fish, and it is an early one too.

When it was new, it would have looked spectacular with the different enamel colours and the bronzed finish, but they did have some strange ideas about what animals made an attractive brooch, didn't they?

My 35th item is yet another type of Roman Brooch, this time a Hod Hill Type Brooch and described as being Romano British, it is tinned bronze and dated to the 1st century.

This was reported to Scunthorpe FLO at the time and was not entered into the database for some reason.

A Hod Hill type tinned brooch with a segmented arched bow with a small central plate decorated with a single Longitudinal ridge. The pin is partially preserved and the catch plate is missing, otherwise it is still fairly solid even though it doesn't look it!

The brooch still shows the silvering and not a common find in Lincolnshire.

Hod Hill Brooches probably originated in the Moselle region, Gaul, during the reign of Augustus (27 BC – 14 AD). Most of these found in Britain are thought to have been brought over during and immediately after the Roman invasion, although some may have arrived earlier. They were superseded by native British types within 20 years.

189

My 36th item is another different Brooch, this time a late Iron Age/Early Roman bronze Langton Down type Brooch dating from the 1st century AD and found near to Market Rasen.

Once again, it was handed over to Scunthorpe FLO and this was also not entered into the database.

Most of these brooches have a cylindrical spring cover with openings at each end and through a slit on the reverse of the cover. This cover seems intact. The top of the spring cover is decorated with incised lines which follow down the body of the brooch. The bow should be flat, but in this instance it has been damaged in antiquity. The bow tapers slightly to the end and although bent, most is still there. The catch plate is missing, as is the pin. There is a fair amount of corrosion along the brooch and it has a browny/green patina.

My 37th find of the decade is the most colourful of all my Roman Brooches! This is an Umbonate Brooch dating from 100-200 AD.

The FLO report says:

An incomplete copper alloy Roman enamelled umbonate brooch. The brooch is domed and covered with two concentric rings of small triangular cells. The outer ring cells are, alternatively, filled with white and blue enamel. The inner triangular cells are narrower and inlaid with white and red enamel. A small conical hollow at the centre shows no trace of enamel. The hinged pin and the stub of the catch plate extend beyond the back. The reverse of the dome is concave-shaped. A part of the pin lug and the catch plate have been preserved. The pin is missing.

The workmanship of these brooches is just amazing and to survive for 2000 years in this condition says something about the people who made them!

This would have been just beautiful when new, and the person who lost it must have been devastated!

My 38th find is a bronze Antoninianus (nummus) of Saloninus dated to 258-260 AD.

This is the only coin from this emperor I have found and this is why it has been included, plus the fact that he was emperor for just two years makes the coin a little rarer.

Obverse shows Radiate draped bust facing right, SALON VALERIANVS CAES.

Reverse shows Sacrificial implements: lituus, Knife, vase turned left, simpulum and aspergillum. PIETAS AVGG.

Publius Licinius Cornelius Saloninus Valerianus was just called Saloninus, he was a Roman nobleman who briefly became Emperor in 260 AD. The grandson of Valerian I, he was appointed Caesar in 258 AD in an attempt to shore up the Licinial line of succession during the crisis of the third century. He administered the German Marches out of Cologne. He soon became embroiled in a dispute with future Caesar of the Gallic Empire Postumus over war spoils. In 260 AD, his troops acclaimed him emperor in a failed bid for political legitimacy, but Postumus killed Saloninus shortly afterwards.

My 39th item of the decade is another rarity, it is a Saxon Brooch dated to 450-550 AD.

The FLO Report is as follows:

An Anglo-Saxon copper alloy Small Long Brooch. The brooch has a flat square head plate decorated with three semi-circular wings. The head plate is decorated with an incised perimeter and a row of punched chevrons down either side. The bow is arched, faceted and decorated with a row of inward-pointing punched chevrons. The panel below the bow tapers and is broken just before it flares into a triangular foot. The foot is also decorated with a perimeter of punched chevrons. There is iron corrosion on the reverse covering the pin lug. The catch plate is intact.

As this is a very special find to me, it had to be included in this book. Apparently, this style of brooch was commonly worn by women during this period and often found in graves.

My 40th find of this decade is a Roman bronze Radiate of Tetricus 1 Dated to 270-3 AD.

The FLO report is a little Sketchy but it is a very worn coin!

Obverse description: Bust of Tetricus facing right

Obverse inscription: (…) ICUS (…)

Reverse description: unknown reverse type

Reverse inscription: Illegible.

I included this particular coin for a couple of reasons really, firstly because of the lack of corrosion, there is just one spot which we hopefully can keep an eye on. Secondly and more importantly, the FLO couldn't find a matching reverse! So that makes it very much a rare coin.

Gaius Pius Esuvius Tetricus was the emperor of Gallic Empire from 271-274 AD. He became emperor after the murder of Victorinus in 271 AD, with the support of Victorinus's mother Victoria. But his reign didn't last long as he was forced to hand over power to his son Tetricus II and he then passed away from natural causes a few years later.

My 41st find is a Roman silver siliqua of Theodosius dated to 378-402 AD.

The FLO report is as follows:

A Clipped Roman silver siliqua of the House of Theodosius Circa 378-402 AD.

Obverse description: Pearled diadem draped and cuirassed bust right.

Obverse inscription: Illegible

Reverse description: Victory Advancing Left

Reverse inscription: Illegible

Obviously the inscriptions have been taken away when clipped but I added this to show that clipping silver coins was also a problem in Roman times as well as in Medieval Times.

I have been lucky, as most of my Roman coins were not clipped, but 95% of bronze ones are corroded!

They are still nice to find!

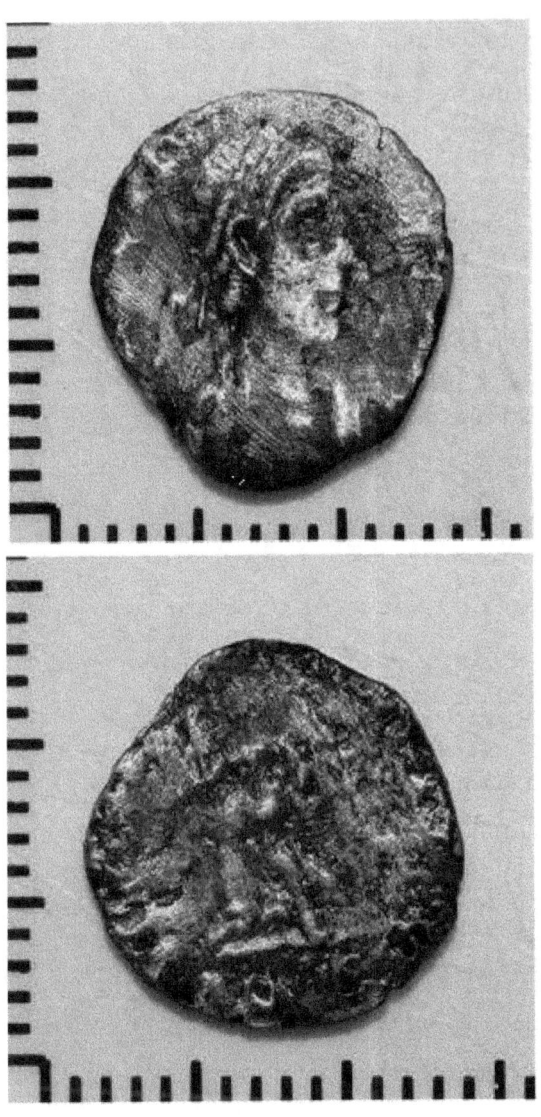

My 42nd find is yet another lovely Roman silver Denarius this time of Hadrian identified by our FLO in Lincoln.

Dated to 121 AD exactly.

The report says:

A Roman silver Denarius of Hadrian

Obverse description: Laureate bust right.

Obverse inscription: IMP CAESAR TRAIAN HADRIANVS AVG

Reverse description: Hadrian seated left on platform, extending right hand to citizen standing right on ground before him.

Reverse inscription: P M TR P COS III; LIBERAL AVG III

Struck in Rome.

The reason for including this coin is that it is silver, it is Hadrian and it is a lovely coin, very proud to save it from our soil!

203

My 43rd item is another silver coin, but this time it is a lot newer!

It is a silver Three Pence from Victoria dated 1899.

As items newer than 300 years old do not need recording, they are mainly just handed back to the finder, as was this. But they are still a part of our history, they are silver and they are really nice to find.

Obverse description: Crowned and veiled head left

Obverse inscription: VICTORIA DEI GRA BRITT REGINA FID DEF IND IMP

Reverse description: Crown in Centre over Large 3 with Date either side of the 3, surrounded by laurel leaves.

I think as time goes on, silver items like this will go over 300 years old and the person/s that found them will be held responsible to report them again, otherwise they may be breaking the law wouldn't they?

Queen Anne and George I coins already fall into that bracket, but for me, detecting 30 years, they would not have been recorded originally, but they should be now!

My 44th find of the decade is a silver Threepence of Elizabeth I dated to 1578-9 AD.

The FLO report says:

Obverse description: Unclear Bust left

Obverse inscription: ELIZABETH DG(ANG FR ET HIB) REGINA

Reverse description: Long Cross over square shield

Reverse inscription: (POSVI DEV ADIVTOREM MEV)

I have mentioned before, many times that the Elizabeth I coins are noted for being poorly minted, particularly the Obverse Heads.

This one is no different and very poorly minted.

It is also very worn too, which doesn't help either.

The main point here is that it is silver and it is still classed under the treasure code as being over 300 years old and more importantly I saved it from even more wear and tear!

207

My 45th find of the decade is a Medieval lead spindle whorl.

Spindle whorls were used as weights on a handheld distaff or spinning stick. They are a common find for metal detectorists. The majority of whorls were made from stone or recycled pots but some, like this one, are made from lead.

Spindle Whorls have been in use since the Iron Age when they used stone; these are probably not shown on the database. Then, in the Roman period, they used ceramic shards and stones. Lead examples started being used in the 10th century and were used through to the late medieval period.

209

My 46th find I have included just because it is an unusual item and not often found in the UK. It is a Manilla, which is a bracelet, in this case made of bronze, and these were used as a form of money from West Africa.

These originated before the colonial period, maybe to trade with the Portuguese Empire. Manillas continued to serve as money and decorative objects until the late 1940s and are still sometimes used as decoration. In popular culture, they are particularly associated with the Atlantic Slave Trade.

They are usually horseshoe-shaped, with terminations that face each other and are roughly lozenge-shaped. The earliest use of manillas was in West Africa, probably originating in Calabar.

I know the subject of slaves annoys thousands of people all over the world and rightly so, but this item may not have been used by a slave, it just could have been an item of adornment and a part of world history.

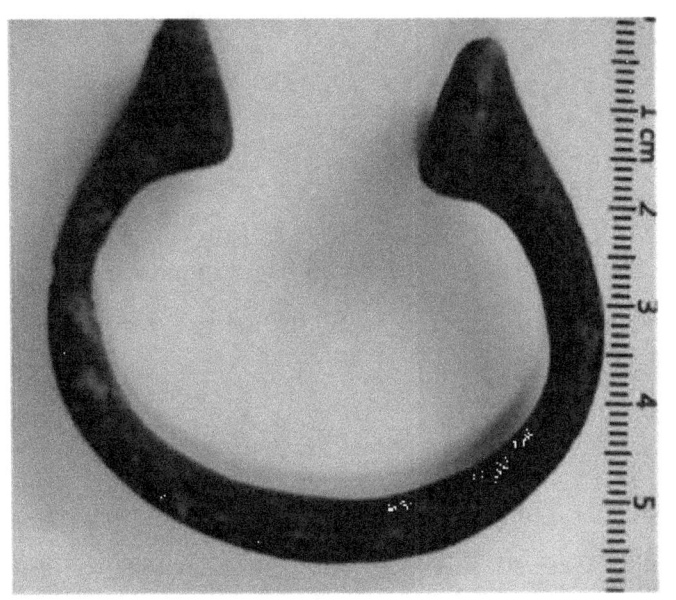

My 47th find in this section is a common find for us detectorists, but this one is special due to its condition. We normally find any Georgian coin either worn out or corroded, but this one has survived really well.

It is a George III Copper Halfpenny dated to 1806.

Obverse description: Laurelled head facing Right

Obverse inscription: GEORGIUS III D G REX

Reverse description: Britannia Facing left, trident in left hand, shield with union flag resting on left, olive branch in raised right hand, sea behind with ship on left.

Reverse inscription: BRITANNIA across the top

A lot of people just put these finds in boxes and they never see the light of day, but some of them are worth showing. George III was never portrayed in a good way in recent times, but he is still a part of our history and should be shared.

213

My 48th find is another Roman coin, this time a bronze nummus of Licinius dating to 313-4 AD.

The FLO from Lincoln report is as follows:

A Late Roman copper alloy nummus of Licinius I Minted in London

Obverse description: Laureate and cuirassed bust right

Obverse inscription: IMP LICINIVS P F AVG

Reverse description: Genius standing left, patera in right hand, cornucopia in left.

Reverse inscription: GENIO-POP ROM

Valerius Licinianus Licinius was a Roman Emperor from 308-324 AD. For most of his reign he was the colleague and rival of Constantine I, with whom he co-authored the "Edict of Milan" in 313 AD, that granted official toleration to Christians in the Roman Empire. He was finally defeated at the Battle of Chrysopolis (324 AD) and was later executed on the orders of Constantine I.

This coin has a little bronze disease in a couple of places but the rest is really clear, far better than most Roman bronzes that come up.

215

My penultimate find of this decade is a Roman silver Denarius of Marcus Aurelius dating back to 155-6 AD.

The Database Report is as follows:

A Roman silver Denarius struck for Marcus Aurelius as Caesar (138-161 AD)

Dating to 155-156 AD, minted in Rome.

Obverse description: Bare Headed and draped bust right.

Obverse inscription: AVRELIVS CAES ANTON AVG PII F

Reverse description: Aequitas standing left holding scales and rod

Reverse inscription: TR POT X COS II

Marcus Aurelius Antoninus was born in Rome in April 121 AD, became Emperor 161 AD. He married Faustina Junior and had 14 children.

Marcus died at the age of 58 of unknown causes in Sirmium and is buried in Hadrian's Mausoleum.

My final find of the noughties is yet another Roman silver Denarius, this time of Trajan, dating back to 98-117 AD.

The FLO report is as follows:

A silver Denarius of Trajan (98-117 AD) Minted in Rome

Obverse description: Laureate head of Trajan right, with light drapery on far shoulder

Obverse inscription: (IMP TR)AIANO AVG GER DAC P M TR (P)

Reverse description: Pax standing left. Holding olive branch and resting on column

Reverse inscription: COS V P P S P(Q R) OPTIMO PRINC

Dated to exactly 109 AD.

Marcus Ulpius Traianus was born in September 53 AD. He became emperor in 98-117 AD married Pompeia Plotina, and had 2 children. He died in 117 AD from Edema at Selinus. His Ashes are beneath Trajan's Column.

219

On completion of the noughties, it was nice to note some really eye-catching finds came up, either eyes only or using a metal detector. As I was not able to search any land for nearly half of the decade due to not gaining permission and due to a heavy workload and a HUGE garden, I think it was a successful decade.

The total finds for the decade were 90 coins and 114 artefacts.

So a lot less than the first decade, but this was to be expected, the finds though were still very nice and varied. I am grateful that I was the person to handle them after so long in the soil.

The time span of these finds from Cretaceous Period, Neolithic, Iron Age, Roman, Saxon all the way through to Victorian times. This hobby is truly amazing.

I look forward to showing you the beautiful finds from Lincolnshire from the 2010s next.

The 2010s

The 2010s have been absolutely amazing for me as far as the different finds are concerned. Once I had gained permission in and around our local area, the finds just kept coming up, Some rare, Some valuable and some very old!

I Invested in the XP Deus when it came onto the market and because it was extremely light and had no connecting wires, and I didn't need to keep changing the batteries as it was rechargeable! I found it an excellent machine to use and ultra-sensitive in finding the smallest items.

Also during this period, I was, once again extremely fortunate in gaining permission on new land, in doing so I stumbled across a previously unknown Roman site, within 10 miles of my home! So you may guess there will be quite a few of these Roman items in this section.

Unfortunately, nowadays I have arthritis in my feet, knees, hips, hands and fingers. It is difficult to detect for long periods, But as I am now retired, I can pick the days I go out as long as the fields are available.

For those people, I may have helped to start up the

hobby, enjoy it for as long as you are able and you will always have help close at hand for anything you find, either from your local FLO Officer or online where you can find help with virtually anything.

But remember, you do need land and permission before you start detecting or unless you are a member of a good, reliable local club.

Good luck and I hope you enjoy these finds from the 2010s.

Because I did!

Apologies in advance if the photos are not quite up to the mark, I am improving!

The 1st item in my 3rd decade of detecting is a one-off for me. A WWI medal was found in a grass field near Wragby.

When I found it I couldn't see any markings at all and only with cleaning, did I start to see that it was a medal and who it was awarded to.

I contacted our local FLO in Lincoln and he was sitting next to a researcher whose speciality was finding relatives alive today.

Within a couple of weeks we had traced the family trees of the owner of the medal, his army career, his sickness whilst serving and his living relatives. To whom we found were still living near Wragby and we organised to return the medal to the family. All within a month of finding the medal.

The only thing we couldn't put together is why his medal ended up in a small grass Field a few miles away from where he last lived, and why there was just one, as everyone from the Great War received at least two, I believe. With the help from our FLO, I found this research really interesting; it made the newspapers and online local news too, and we got to shake hands with his only living relative!

My 2nd item from the 2010s is a tiny cut silver farthing of William I dated from 1083-6 AD identified as Type 1269.

William the Conqueror, was the First Norman Monarch of England, reigning from Christmas Day (Which was the day he was crowned King of England) 1066, following his victory over Harold Godwinson at Hastings, until his death in 1087.

William was the son of the unmarried Duke Robert 1 of Normandy and his Mistress Herleva, hence his other name, "William the Bastard".

He did marry Matilda of Flanders in the 1050s and, between them, had at least eight children two of which were to become Kings of England, William II and Henry I.

We do not find many cut farthings but this one is a special one to me.

My 3rd item In this section is another rare and unusual coin to be found in Lincolnshire. The stars in the quarter sections on the reverse are a giveaway, it being Scottish. So this is a cut silver halfpenny of William the 1st of Scotland dating to 1165-70 AD.

William the Lion, or the Garbh (Rough), Reigned as King of Scots from 1165 to 1214 AD. The second longest reign in Scottish History behind James VI which was the longest.

Strangely, William was born in Huntingdon in 1142 during the reign of his Grandfather, King David I.

He married Ermengarde de Beaumont in 1186 and had 4 children, one of which would become Alexander II of Scotland.

These coins all tell a story if you find time to investigate.

My 4th find from this decade is one of the oldest coins I have ever found. It is a pre-invasion silver Denarius minted by Vibius of Pansa dating to 90 BC, so it would have been 130 years old before the Romans invaded Britain. There must be a story behind it being in the fields of Lincolnshire, my feeling is that one of the invaders brought it with them as a legacy, like we do today, a keepsake from times past. But I could be completely wrong, of course.

Obverse: PANSA—Laureate Head of Apollo Facing Right

Reverse: C.VIBIVS CF– Minerva in Quadriga right

Gaius Vibius Pansa Caetronianus was Consul of the Roman Republic in 43 BC. He supported Julius Caesar during the Civil War, and pushed for the restoration of the Republic after Caesar's death.

Pansa was the first in his family to serve in the Roman Senate and to be elected Consul and served under Julius Caesar in Gaul.

He died of his injuries received in the Battle of Forum Gallorium in 43 BC. Needless to say it is a special find of mine and another one off!

My 5th find of the 2010s is another silver Denarius, this time of Vespasian dating from 69-71 AD. It is a little worn, but otherwise in good condition.

Obverse: IMP CAESAR VESPASIANVS AVVG Laureate Head Right

Reverse: COS ITER-TR POT Pax seated left, branch upward in right hand, caduceus in left. Rome Mint.

Titus Flavius Vespasianus (which was his full name) was born in Falacrine in 9 AD. He reigned as Emperor from 69-79 AD. The 4th and last emperor who reigned in the year of the four Emperors. He founded the Flavian Dynasty that ruled the empire for 27 years. His fiscal reforms and consolidation of the empire generated political stability and a huge Roman building program.

He married Domitilla the elder (who died before 69 AD) after which he married his Mistress Caenis. He had three children Titus, Domitilla the Younger and Domitian. He also participated in the invasion of Britain. He died in 79 AD and was buried in Rome.

My 6th find of this decade is a really unique find from the Lincolnshire fields, or probably any English fields, come to that.

It is a silver seal top spoon end from the makers, Julius Hollister of New York, dated 1846. It was found in a tiny Acre Field and one must ask, why would it be here?

This was identified by our local FLO, and he was also so surprised he wanted to log it into the National Database.

Seal Top Spoons have been in use in Britain since Elizabethan times, and they are very collectible nowadays.

It is a shame that this one was broken when I found it, but we can't have everything, can we?

Definitely is one of my most unusual finds...

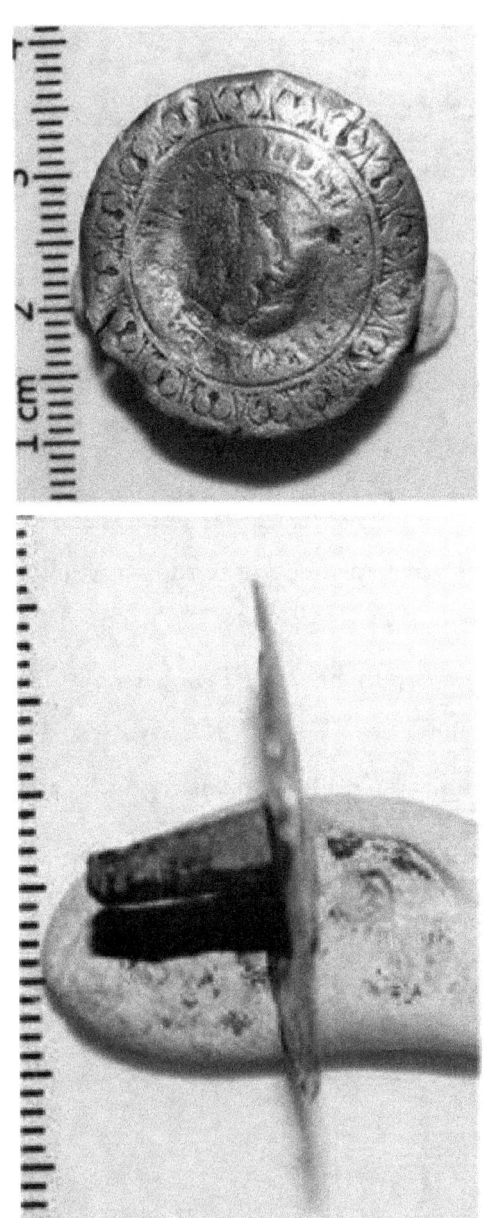

235

My 7th find from this decade is a copper alloy Saxon Scabbard Chape, and reported by our local FLO as follows:

Plain sheet metal terminal with a rounded end and folded to conical form, and with flattened broader sides. There are six rings and dots on the chape but sadly there is only one side remaining.

This chape is dated broadly between 410 and 1100 AD.

To find a chape in good condition would be really nice, but to find a Saxon Chape in Good Condition would be a dream, however I smiled a big smile when I pulled this out of the earth. Saxon artefacts are so hard to find but really nice when you do, no matter what condition they are in.

My 8th find was another item that went through the treasure process and was subsequently returned back to me, for which I was grateful.

This is a Roman Finger Ring Bezel that had come apart from the ring itself. It consists of a Carved Carnelian stone embedded in a silver setting, which is why it was classed as treasure in the first place.

The FLO report states it is a Roman silver box bezel containing a carnelian intaglio. The bezel stands 7 mm tall. The gem is oval in form with a polished convex face, engraved with a motif of a male figure standing frontally but facing left, holding an ear of wheat in his lowered left hand and offering out patera in his outstretched right. There is a small chip in the gem towards its apex, between the figure's chin and outstretched arm. The figure can be identified as Bonus Eventus, the Roman personification of "good outcome". Bonus Eventus is the most popular motif found in intaglios from Roman Britain. With over 120 recovered so far!

Dated between 155 to 300 AD

239

I have been very lucky to find a large amount of pottery on my Roman field and so far, it has filled a shopping bag.

My Ninth find of this decade shows that there was an important building close by, as it is the best Samian ware that Romans used.

The report from the FLO states:

A Roman pottery fragment of a Samian ware bowl. It is the incomplete base of a shallow bowl. All that remains is a small part of the pedestal foot and the body, with a slight curve forming the base of the bowl. The fabric is a light orange-pink colour with the slip being a dark orange-red. Evidence of it being wheel-turned is on the base of the vessel. There is a feathered patterned band 21mm in from the base rim.

They never dated it other than saying it is from the Roman Period.

By collecting all the pottery as you walk around detecting, a picture can be put together as to how long they were in use.

241

My 10th item is another Roman copper alloy item, it is a nail cleaner and more than likely one of a set of items that were carried together on a Chatelaine.

The FLO Report states:

A Roman, copper alloy, plain nail cleaner with a straight-sided blade. The object is long and rectangular and then has a broken suspension loop at the top of the cleaner. The cleaner has a green and brown patina. The object is slightly bent, however, only damage is to the loop.

The nail cleaner is dated to 43-200 AD.

These items we find, go to prove that they very much lived their lives as we do and they each had things handy to use in their everyday lives.

This is one of the reasons we do this, bringing history to life.

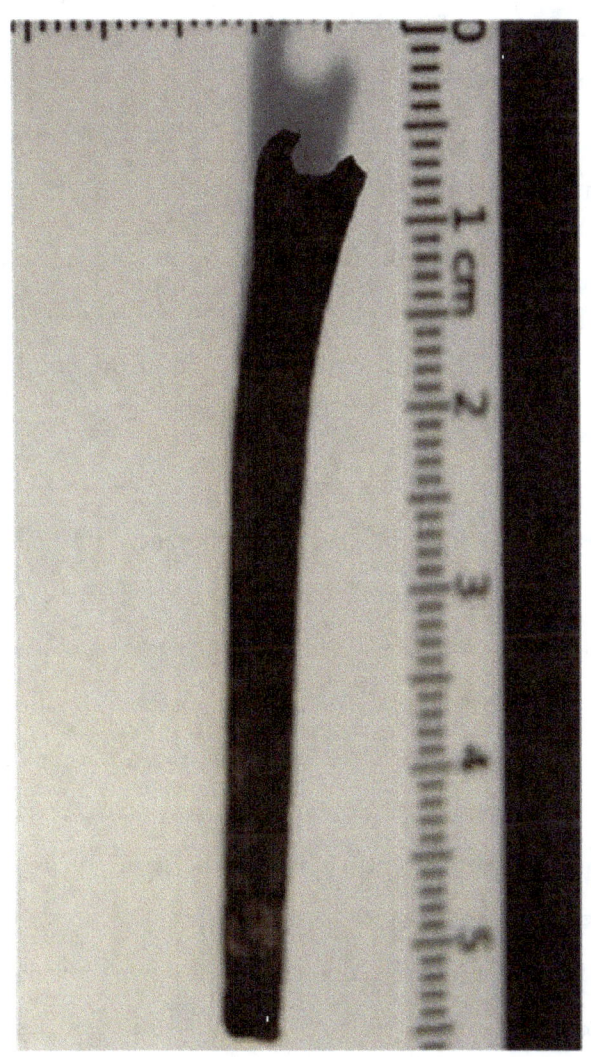

My 11th find is once again from my Roman Field and an unusual one too. It shows that the Romans also played games or gambled, although this Lead Roman dice is a bit crude, to say the least. But I love it, just couldn't believe it when I found it.

The report by the FLO says: A Lead Die, the object is a square in plan and rectangular in section, and each panel contains dots representing one of the numbers between 1-6.

The die is crudely made and has uneven corners and edges. The number one is represented by a single dot in the centre of one of the two larger faces. To the right the panel is decorated with four dots, one on each corner. To the right, the panel is decorated with six dots, three along each side. To the right, the panel is decorated with three dots set diagonally across the face from top left to bottom right. The panel on top is decorated with five dots arranged in two lines. The panel at the base is decorated with two dots both located in the bottom right corner. So the basic design is the same as a dice today.

A Lovely thing to find though...

My 12th item is a Roman bronze Votive Offering of Minerva as described by our local FLO, and dated to 2nd-3rd century.

The description from the finds Liaison Officer is as follows:

A cast Roman copper alloy mount in the form of the goddess Minerva. The object is in a good state of preservation, although the surface is rather worn and pitted, obscuring some of the finer details. The face of Minerva is particularly worn, but the general mouldings clearly show that she is life-like, facing forward with hair visible beneath the helmet along the forehead, and the hair goes around the sides of the head. Her nose has been lost, through wear and corrosion. Minerva wears a high Corinthian helmet with a large crest, which has a groove across the top and tapering sides. Minerva was the goddess of Wisdom and Learning. Another one off for me!

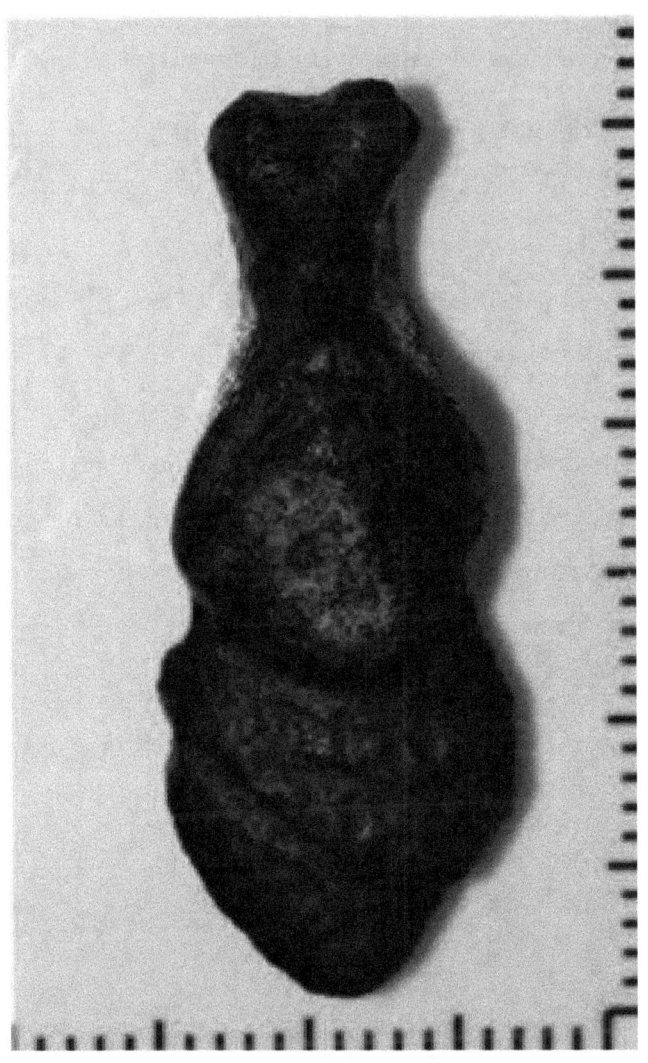

My 13th find of this decade is yet another Roman find from the previously unknown field. It Is a bronze Umbonate brooch in a lovely condition as you can see.

The report from our FLO is as follows:

A Roman copper alloy Umbonate brooch with a pin and catch plate missing, dating from 45 to 200 AD. From the central recessed dot on the boss, triangular cells fan out in a sunburst fashion, and there are 14 cells on the outer ring. Some cells have traces of silvering and some are decorated with blue enamel. The boss has a diameter of 20mm. There is one large lug for the spring, opposite the missing catch plate. The head of which widens out into a collar.

This field has given me so much pleasure from the finds that have appeared from it, and this is one of the best!

249

My 14th find was found in the field adjacent to the Roman Site and when I found it, I immediately thought it was from a Roman statuette but when I showed it to the FLO he thought differently as per his report:

A cast copper alloy fragment of a figurine or statuette, probably of the crucified Christ. If this identification is correct, the figurine is likely to be medieval in date. The fragment comprises the left hand above the wrist. The fragment is likely cast and the fingers moulded into position. The fingers of the hand are extended and the thumb is slightly curved round, leaving a gap between the thumb and forefinger. The nails on three of the four fingers are visible. The hand is a mid-greenish brown colour. A linear channel is visible across the break at the wrist. The channel is concave and probably represents a rivet hole. The location of this rivet hole through the wrist suggests that this is a crucifix figurine. The break is patinated, suggesting damage in antiquity. Dated 1200-1500 AD. But I still think it is Roman!

Love it!

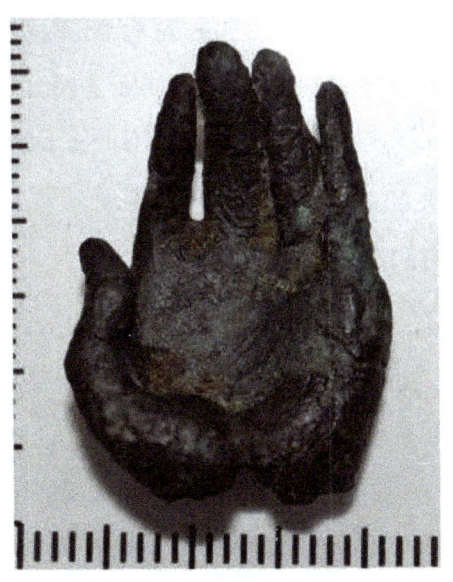

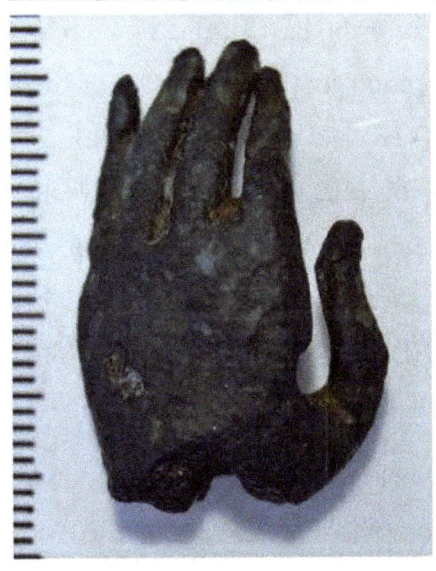

My 15th find of the decade is another medieval silver item that I thought would go through the treasure process. It is a medieval silver hawking bell found near Wragby.

The FLO report is as follows:

An incomplete silver bell dating to the post-medieval period (1500-1900 AD) composite. The hollow upper and lower halves were originally soldered together. A series of grooves decorate the upper half of the bell, running around the upper half vertically radiating from the base of the, now broken soldered wire suspension loop. The bell is now distorted and broken. There are no surviving marks. Small bells similar to this were in use from the 16th century as dress accessories and hawking bells, but it may date anywhere from the 16th to the 20th centuries. Therefore, because it cannot be dated to before 1700, it has not been reported as treasure.

These bells do not come up very often and only two similar ones have been recorded on the PAS database.

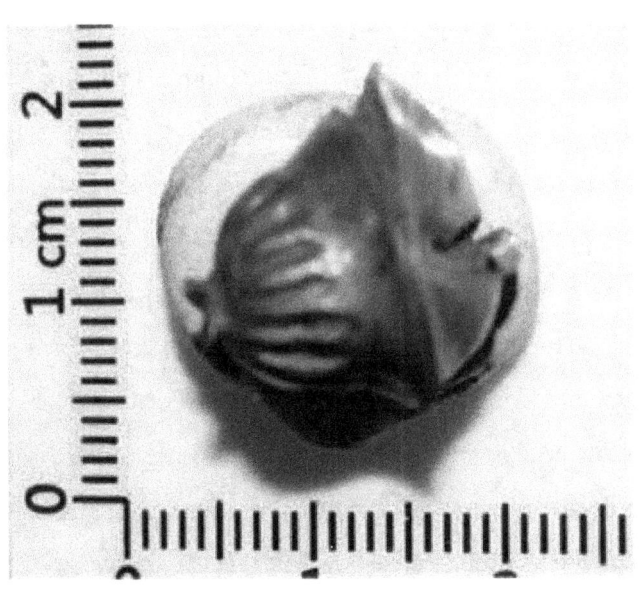

My 16th item is yet another Roman object made of bronze, it is a horse's head mount and really solid too.

The FLO report states:

A Roman copper alloy mount in the form of a horse's head, which emerges from a flat backplate. The head is shown in three dimensions, and details are shown by a combination of fine mouldings and incised lines. The neck is pointed oval in section and tapers to the head. The head is shown semi-naturalistically. It has pointed ears, behind both of which is a pair of incised crescents, presumably representing folds in the skin. The horse has thick brow ridges, below which is a pointed oval eye with a recessed pellet centre. The snout is elongated and terminates with two recessed pellets representing the nostrils. The mouth is open, which gives the head as a whole a sense of energy and movement, somewhat as if the horse is galloping. The same motion is indicated by the mane at the top of the head, which sweeps backwards. This was dated 43-410 AD, so the whole time of Roman occupation!

This find was one of a few that the farmer wanted to keep, but at least I have the photos.

My 17th find is yet another Roman bronze mount, this time of a Chicken. Once again, from the field adjacent to the Roman site.

The report from our FLO is:

A Roman copper alloy object in the form of a cockerel. The bird is shown in three dimensions. It has a thin, narrow head with a flat, rounded panel of copper alloy extending from the base of the chin to its neck. It is unclear whether this is intentional, or if it is waste that has not been trimmed off. The body flares to a pointed oval base. The tail is represented by a large, curved panel of copper alloy rising from the pointed end. The underside of the bird is hollow, and an integral bar extends from side to side. An incomplete rectangular stub of copper alloy extends from the base of the chest, and a circular stub extends from the tail end. The surface is highly corroded; the function is not clear, it could be a vessel mount or a manicure set.

This was dated from 43-250 AD.

We just do not know what else is hidden in these fields!

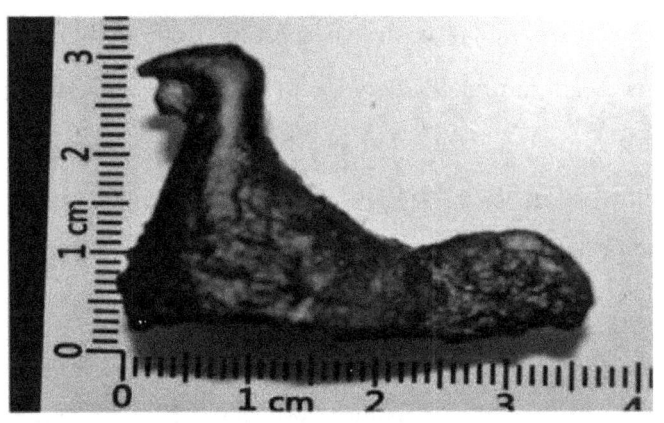

My 18th find Is another rare Roman mount in a totally different field. This time it is of a Bull! The report is as follows:

An almost complete cast copper alloy Roman zoomorphic figurine in the form of a Bull (43-410 AD). The animal appears to have been cast hollow. It is in a recumbent position, shown in profile to the right, with its head turned 90 degrees to the body and facing forward. It is truncated on the opposite side and is finished with a flat rim that would have abutted another object. The hollow part is filled with lead alloy, but this is at a slightly lower level than the rim. Approximately half the bull survives. The figurine is broken in a rough manner vertically across the body. The break is patinated, suggesting that it broke in antiquity. The body is muscular, and along the belly are two or three grooves. The incomplete right foreleg is turned inwards and rests in a horizontal position so that the hock is parallel to the body. The bull has been given three horns. Very few other bronze bulls are known from Britain, this could have been made here or in Gaul. A three-horned bull was a sign of strength.

A similar one was found in 1924 in the Lexden tumulus near Colchester 15-10BC suggesting the grave was for a king called Addedomaros. Another rarity!

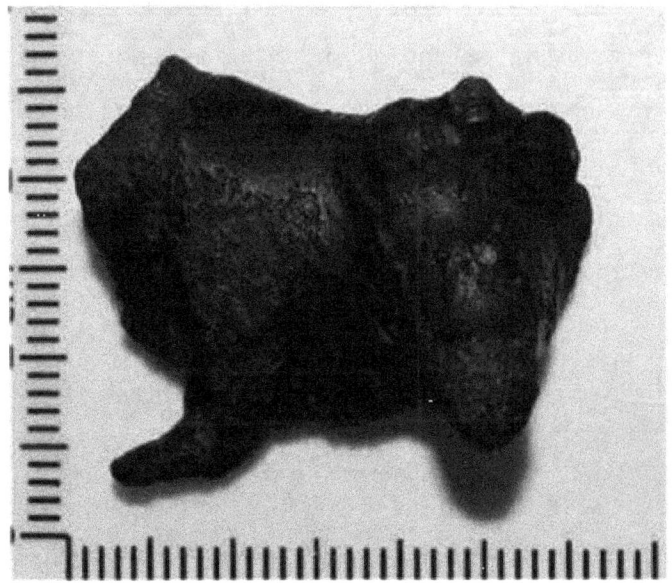

My 19th find is a Roman bronze Bird mount from the same field as the Chicken mount and dated to 43-410 AD.

The report for this find by our FLO is as follows:

A Roman copper alloy zoomorphic mount. The mount is in the shape of a sitting bird with both wings resting at its side. The eyes look as if they were carved into the sides after casting and the beak is straight but slightly hooked down. There is a straight line down the centre from the bottom to the neck to the tail.

There is a hole in the base of the mount that would have originally been where it would have been secured to its vessel. A small trace of iron corrosion is visible within the hole on the base. The left side of the neck and right wing of the bird have some scratches indented on the surface and there are some white spots on the back and right side of the neck.

Another lovely find from one of the most famous periods in our history.

I think it is a Pigeon!

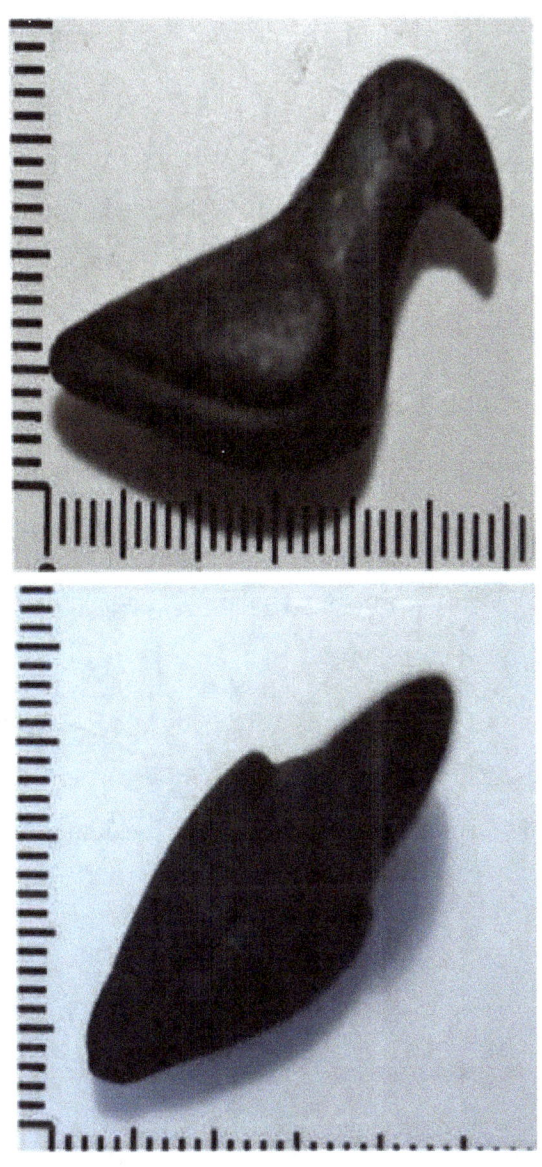

261

My 20th find of this decade is a jetton, and an unusual one at that.

It is a copper alloy German jetton from Hans Krauwinckel I dated from 1562-1586 AD, and called the "Lion of St Mark" type.

Obverse Description: "Orb"

Inscription: HANS KRAVWINCKEL NVRE

Reverse Description: "Lion of St Mark"

Inscription: S MARCVS EVANGELLI ()GOT()

It is very worn, but you can see the design and some of the wording.

These types of jettons were made by a few different makers, which cover different periods. There are six jettons of the Lion of St Mark type, including the one shown here.

Although I have several jettons from Germany, this is the only one of this type I have found, to date!

My 21st find of the decade is another rare early Roman silver Denarius, this time of the moneyer Naevius Balbus, minted in Rome 79BC.

The report states a Roman silver Republican Denarius

Obverse: Head of Apollo Right,

Reverse: Uncertain animal advancing right (I think it is Victory in Triga)

These particular coins are normally serrated on the edge, this one may either be a freak or very worn!

The name Naevius was generally regarded as a patronymic surname derived from a birthmark. Balbus was a common surname originally to one who stammers.

It is hard to believe that this was struck 120 years before they invaded Britain, which makes it another one-off for me!

My 22nd find is a really unusual one made of copper alloy, this is a modified medieval jetton made into a brooch.

The FLO reports it as an incomplete medieval copper alloy nummular brooch adapted from a jetton. The perimeter of the jetton is damaged in places, and both sides are very worn. The upper surface is decorated with a triple-stranded cross. The other side is equally worn, but a feint inner circle is visible, as are faint, illegible letters. An attachment mechanism is riveted to the jetton through the centre, using a copper alloy rivet. This mechanism takes the form of a narrow tapering strip of sheet copper alloy with a recurving sharp hook at one end, while the other end has an attachment loop formed by rolling the metal into a cylinder that spirals inwards towards the plate.

This is dated to 1200-1300 AD.

My 23rd find has got to be a one off! It is a medieval lead squirrel badge dating between 1200-1500 AD.

The FLO report says: A medieval lead badge in the form of a squirrel. The squirrel is shown crouching on the floor. Its front paws hold a nut in its mouth. The body of the squirrel is slender, and tapers to the neck. It is decorated with a series of small pellets, with a row of moulded diagonal lines running along its back. The feet are also elongated and similarly decorated with moulded diagonal lines. The face is oval and the eye is shown by a single pellet. The ears rise vertically from the head: both are decorated with a small groove down the centre. A nut, defined by a large pellet, is shown in its mouth. The tail is slender and extends along its back and up to its ears. The tail is decorated with a series of moulded chevrons. A casting seam runs along the centre of the back. Two incomplete swellings are seen on the reverse, opposite to the squirrel's rear end. This presumably is the remains of a pin lug. It's very unusual too.

My 24th find of this decade is the best Seal Matrix I have found to date.

The report is as follows: A medieval copper-alloy seal matrix. The handle is hexagonally faceted and tapers to a quatrefoil-shaped loop at the apex. The face of the seal depicts the head of a stag facing, with a cross between the antlers. The inscription surrounding this reads LELSV.

The stag and cross-device is used in the heraldic arms of St Eustace and St Hubert of Liege (Patron saint of Huntsmen), who saw a stag with a cross between its antlers while out hunting. St Eustace had the same vision. This is a generic seal matrix rather than a personal one; during the 14th century, the use of nonheraldic motifs and personal legends became popular.

This particular Seal Matrix is dated 1300-1400 AD and in really nice condition.

271

This is a very rare item, in that it went to the local FLO and was returned from them, but no report was forthcoming.

It is so nice and unusual that it had to be included in this section.

It is copper alloy and classed as Horse furniture, more likely a Horse Harness Boss.

When new, it would be like gold as it is bronze with inserts all over of blue and white enamel. There must be over 80 in total but unfortunately, some have fallen out in antiquity, which is a big shame.

Dated to the medieval period, this item would have outshone most others of the period.

273

My 26th item is another Roman Denarius, this time alleged to be a copy of Macrinus, who only reigned for two years 217-8 AD.

The original report stated: A copper alloy contemporary copy of a denarius of the emperor Macrinus. Mint of Rome. The style and patina of the coin are unusual and the national finds advisor would need to handle this to determine when it was produced.

Obverse: Laureate bust right

(IMP C) M OPEL SEV MACRINVS AVG

Reverse: Providentia standing in the centre holding a baton above the globe and a cornucopia.

PROVIDENTIA DEORVM

Well I did take this coin down to the British Museum for confirmation and was pleasantly surprised that they agreed it was genuine and very rare as only 5 similar had been recorded anywhere.

They also updated the database recording to confirm this. A very pleasant day in the capital was had too!

275

My 27th find of the 2010s is a copper penny Token of John of Gaunt the Duke of Lancaster, dated to 1791-2.

It is a Complete copper penny of John of Gaunt, Duke of Lancaster. The obverse shows a crowned and robed bust of John of Gaunt facing left. The inscription reads IOHN OF GAUNT DUKE OF LANCASTER. The reverse shows a shield of arms with the motto SIC DONEC on a scroll beneath, and a rosette beneath it all, the inscription reads (PAYABLE BY THOMAS BALL) SLEAFORD.

Thomas Ball was a grocer and ironmonger in Sleaford, Lincolnshire. Several thousand of these tokens were minted for general circulation circa 1794.

So although it is unusual, it is a fairly common token. I like it because of its links to my home county Lincolnshire, and to get a penny Token is a rarity for me.

If it weren't for us Detectorists a lot of our Knowledge would still be hidden or rotting away in the Soils beneath our feet.

My 28th item is also unusual, it is a sterling silver penny of John of Brabant I, dated 1280-1294, so it's early.

The report says: A Complete medieval silver continental copy of an Edwardian sterling penny. Possibly minted 1267-94 AD.

Obverse: (I?DVX?(?)IE?) Bust of King facing forward with a flat crown.

Reverse: DVX BRA BAN TIE , Long cross dividing the inscription with three pellets in each quarter.

John I of Brabant, (also called John the Victorious) was Duke of Brabant, Lothier and Limburg. During the 13th century, John was venerated as a folk hero. He has been painted as the perfect model of a brave, adventurous and chivalrous feudal prince. Born in Leuven, Belgium in 1253. He married Margaret of France, followed by Margaret of Flanders. He fathered eight children. Passing away in Bar-le-Duc, France in 1294 after being mortally wounded in the arm in an encounter with Pierre de Bausner. He was buried in Brussels. It is an unusual find, which is why it is a special one of mine.

My 29th find is also unusual as it is a copper alloy coin weight that has been pierced years later and threaded through for one reason or another, recycled is a word we use today!

The report says: copper alloy possible coin weight. Sub rectangular flat object with a centrally drilled hole of 7.2mm diameter. Which is surrounded by two rings and in between them, there are various patterns of flowers, dots and fleurs-de-lis. The sides of the object are knife-trimmed, presumably to achieve a particular value. The reverse is plain but has a small stamp of a fleur de lis in the corner. Date between 1540-1600 AD.

We have found out since that this was the weight of a gold coin from the period of James I, but trying to pin it to a particular coin is very difficult because the weight is now incorrect due to the hole through the centre.

A rose ryal is a distinct possibility dated to 1619.

Sometimes, finding the artefact is the easiest part!

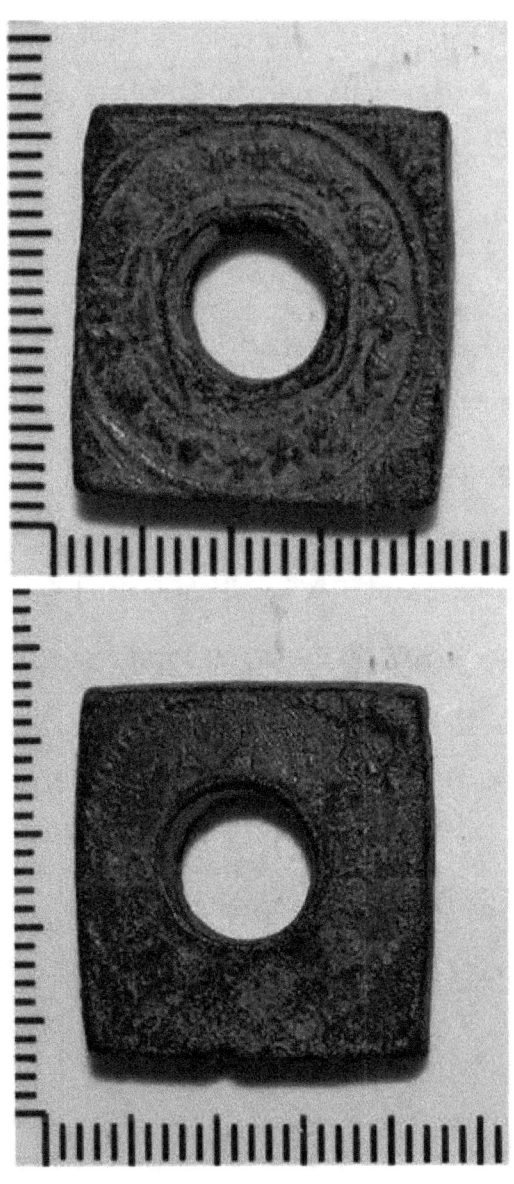

My 30th find of the decade is a lovely little silver penny of Henry VIII dating to 1526-1544 AD.

The report says:

A silver penny of Henry VIII (Bishop Thomas Wolsey), mint of Durham.

Obverse: King enthroned holding orb and sceptre, two double pillars.

Inscription: H D G ROSE SIE SPINA

Reverse: Royal Shield over long cross, which divides the legend. T W beside shield, hat below.

Inscription CIVI TAS DVR RAM

This is the only penny I have for Henry VIII so a very special find which took over 22 years to make. It may not look much, but to me, it is not replaceable.

As for the king's story? Everyone already knows!

My 31st item is another silver Hammered medieval penny, this time of Henry II and in fairly good condition for one of its kind.

The FLO Report says:

A silver penny of Henry II "Tealby Type."

Dated to 1158-1180 AD

Obverse: Crowned bust facing, sceptre in the right hand.

HEN()

Reverse: Cross and Crosslets

()ST()

Although it is very worn, this is what we come to expect with these poorly minted coins, named after a hoard of these pennies, which were found in Tealby Lincolnshire.

one of my favourites!

My 32nd item is by far one of my best coins ever! The condition is immaculate and must have been lost as new! It is a Roman Denarius of Hadrian.

The report is as follows:

A silver Denarius of Hadrian, SALVS AVG (Salus feeding snake arising from the altar, Rome Mint, 137 AD.

Obverse: Laureate Head Right

HADRIANVS AVG COS III P P

Reverse: Salus Feeding a snake arising from an altar

SALVS AVG

Hadrian was emperor from 117-138 AD and is very well known within Britain for building a big wall! He was born into a Roman Italo-Hispanic family, which settled in Spain from the Italian city of Atri. He married Vibia Sabina and had 2 adopted sons, Lucius Aelius Caesar and Antoninus Pius.

Hi died in Baiae, Italy and is buried in Hadrian's Mausoleum in Rome. This is a beautiful coin.

The 33rd find of the decade is another one-off; it is a bronze Georgian Seal Matrix with an amber setting a man's head carved out. This is yet another item I handed in to the FLO's and had it handed back without it being recorded onto the database. This has happened a few times in the past few years, I do worry that we do our job in handing everything in and they don't get recorded.

However, it is obvious as to what it is and what it is made of. The only thing we do not know is who the head is supposed to represent, it does look a little like George III, but my guess is that it is a wealthy trader or landowner of the period.

As to date, possibly 1714-1837, I know it's a large date range, but it is Georgian.

The temptation to clean such items will always be there, but it is best not to.

289

My 34th item is a lovely silver bank token of George III, dated to 1811.

It has been recorded as follows:

A George III silver bank token 1s 6d dated 1811.

Obverse: has the bust laureate right.

GEORGIUS III DEI GRATIA REX

Reverse: Shows a Wreath which surrounds the words on four lines:

BANK, TOKEN, 1s 6D, 1811.

Both sides are marked around the outer edge with an inward facing evenly sized and spaced multi-toothed pattern. The coin is in good condition.

When I found this I never even knew they existed! You will always learn something having a hobby such as this.

My 35th find is yet another copper alloy jetton from France found in the fields of South Lincolnshire.

The original short report on the database said:

A copper alloy French jetton.

Obverse? PILET? LAFET? ?IMIDICL; rose stops; large lis in centre within arched perimeter.

Reverse: CA(V)E– Single stranded cross fleuretty or arches, A V E M in angles. Date medieval 1380-1440 AD.

I wasn't happy with this report at all and contacted the British Museum direct and sent a copy of the photos. They quickly responded that this was a jetton that had not been recorded anywhere or in any books they had!

They have now updated the database and marked it as a find of national importance and a find of note. It has now been reported as A Tournai jetton struck by Michell Pollet 1450-1461

A one-off! Amazing!

It is in remarkable condition for a jetton of this age. Note: if you are not happy with a report, get it checked out, it could be rare!

My 36th item is another lovely Hammered medieval silver coin, this time, it is a half groat (2 Pence) of Edward III.

The report from the PAS Database is as follows:

A Long Cross silver Half Groat of Edward III 1351-1377 AD.

Obverse: Head of King facing forward with a crown bearing fleurs de Lys encircled by a tressure of 9 arches. This is surrounded by inscription +EDW(ARD)US REX ANGL (ZF)

Reverse: A Long Cross with three pellets centrally located in each quadrant, surrounded by the inscription CIVI TAS LON DON PO(SVIDE)VADIVT OREm

Edward III was also known as Edward of Windsor before his accession, was King of England and Lord of Ireland from 1327 until his death in 1377. He is noted for his military success and for restoring royal authority after the disastrous and unorthodox reign of his father, Edward II.

He married Philippa of Hainault and had 8 sons and 5 Daughters.

He died in 1377 following a stroke.

My 37th find came as a complete shock as it is my only Hammered Gold coin to date and I had to wait 30 years to find it!

It is a little bent, but other than that it feels like it was made yesterday.

The report says: A Gold Quarter Noble of Edward III, Treaty Series 1363-1369 AD. 4th Coinage.

Obverse: Shield with Quartered Arms of England and France within a tressure of eight arches, double saltire stops.

EDWARD DEI GRA REX ANGL

Reverse: Floriated cross with a Lys at the end of each limb, in each angle, a lion passant, guardant., all within a tressure of eight arches, double saltire stops.

EXALTABITUR IN GLORIA

It was one of those unforgettable moments, it was cold and wet and very, very muddy! But worth it!

297

My 38th find is also a first for me, a Celtic silver Half Unit from our local tribe, the Corieltavi. It is a shame it was broken in antiquity, but a broken one is better than none at all!

The FLO's Report says:

A north-eastern silver half-unit, boar horse type attributed to the Corieltavi.

Obverse description: Obliterated die

Reverse Description: Horse right, ring of pellets above.

This was dated to 25-50 AD So very close to the Roman invasion and occupation.

The Corieltavi ruled the land from Lincolnshire to Leicestershire and were neighbours to Boudicca's Iceni tribe. It looks as though, at one time, they had multiple rulers covering the region, as the coins had two or three different names inscribed on them. They had an important mint and maybe even a tribal centre at Sleaford.

My 39th find was found about four miles and 9 Years apart from the silver Half unit on the previous page. This Gold Stater from the Corieltavi is in excellent condition and is the only one I have found, to date.

The report from our FLO says:

A late Iron Age gold stater attributed to the Corieltavi. North East Coast type, three-line variety struck 60-20BC

Obverse Description: Wreath crossed by line

Reverse Description: Horse left, pellet star in front, two pellets above, pellet in ring of pellets below.

The finding of this lovely coin was a true golden moment. I can't imagine how one of our former club members felt when she found a hoard of them near her home!

A true once-in-a-lifetime experience, but you still have to walk over it to find it!

My 40th find of this decade is another amazing find, another one-off and a very rare coin. It is a silver shilling of Charles I Minted in Newark Castle and called a siege piece. Apparently, only the second to be reported in our County.

The report is as follows: A post-medieval silver siege piece struck at Newark. The coin is lozenge-shaped and has a circular hole at its apex. The obverse depicts a crown flanked on either side by C & R. The crown has ten dots on the right arch and ten on the left. Below the crown are the numerals XII, which denotes the denomination as a shilling. All these are enclosed by an off-centred lozenge perimeter of pellets. The reverse has the following text placed over three lines: OBS / NEWARK / 1646. The letters are thick, and the inscription is enclosed by a lozenge perimeter of pellets. The surface of the coin is relatively unworn, but the texts and motifs have been stamped onto a surface containing multiple nicks and cut marks, perhaps caused by the silver plate from which the coin has been cut was worked and hammered flat.

This coin made our local newspaper and the story of how Charles's Army in the castle was surrounded by the roundheads and they ran out of money, so they made their own from the silverware within the castle.

To Actually find one is just a mind-blowing event itself! The farmer decided to keep it himself unfortunately!

My 41st find of the decade is another unusual one it is a Roman bronze Phallic pendant dated to the whole of the Roman period they were in Britain. 43-410 AD.

The Report states: copper alloy Pendant. Cast Phallic pendant with two pairs of small round testes below the suspension loop in the centre. Indications are that there were two phallies on either side of the testes, but both are damaged.

This object is so small it must have been a child's pendant and hung around their neck.

These pendants were a symbol of fertility as well as being a charm to protect against evil spells and were a common piece of jewellery in ancient Rome. Apparently charms of this kind were worn by babies and soldiers. This one would have been a baby's for sure!

305

My 42nd item in this section is a bronze Crotal Bell and the best I have found in Lincolnshire in my opinion. The report states:

A post-medieval copper alloy "crotal" bell cast c 1600-1800 AD. The bell is spherical 32 mm in diameter. The upper half has two sound holes 5mm in diameter and the lower sound holes 8mm in diameter. The lower ones are joined together by a slot and are perpendicular to those on the upper half. Both halves of the bell chamber are decorated with a sunburst design. This takes the form of a number of elongated ovoid petals radiating from the centre of the hemisphere. There is a raised rib around the circumference between the two hemispheres. The corroded iron pea moves freely within the bell. The integral suspension loop is of sub-rectangular form with a drilled hole. No maker's mark visible.

I have found several crotal bells, a lot of which do still ring, but I do like this one.

307

My 43rd find of this decade is a Bronze Age flat axe and it was just laid on the surface waiting for me.

The FLOs report states: A worn copper alloy flat axe of the early to middle bronze Age.

The blade end is crescentric in form, flaring to either side of the axe. The cutting edge is damaged in places but otherwise is in good condition. It has a flat, rectangular body that gradually tapers towards the butt end. Halfway along the axe on either side is a shallow stop ridge that seems to be early forms of the more prominent versions seen on palstaves.

The axe has patches of a brownish patina: the surface is smooth and in good condition.

Dated to BC2350-1150.

These are just lovely things to find and you just can't help thinking, what the last person to hold it was actually like!

It just makes you shiver...

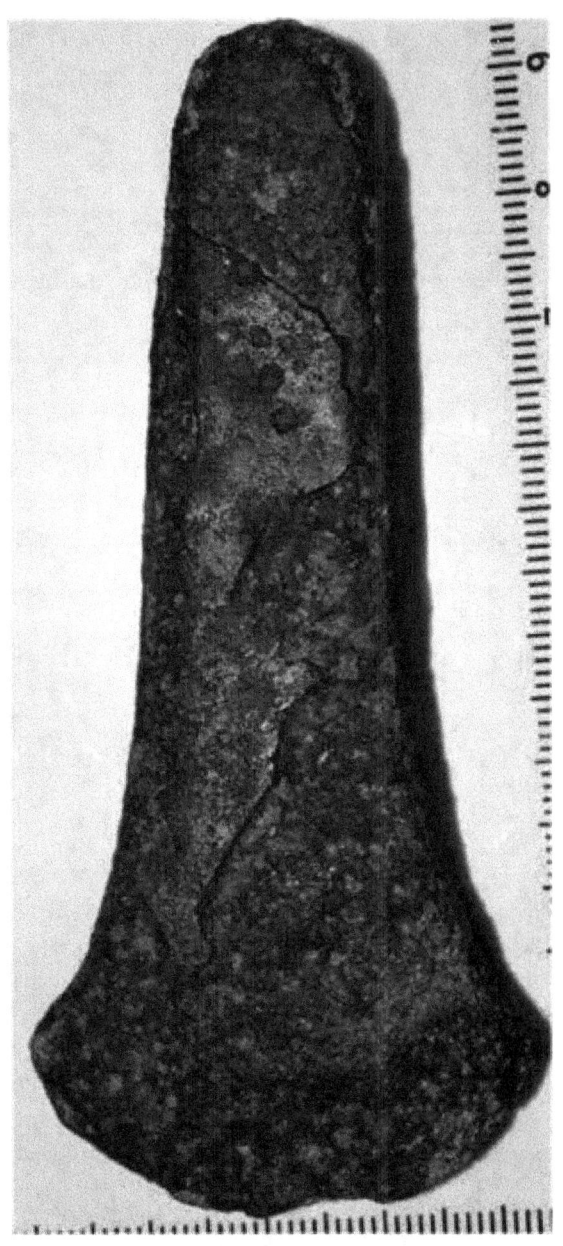

309

My 44th item is another Roman silver Denarius, this time of Augustus Caesar dating to 13BC.

The FLO's report is as follows:

A Roman silver Denarius of Augustus (27 BC-14 AD) of the moneyer C. Antistius Reginus, dating to the period c.13 BC

Obverse Descr: Bare Head Right

Obverse Inscr: CAESAR AVGUSTVS

Reverse Descr: Simpulum and lituus above tripod and patera

Reverse Inscr: (C AN)TISTIVS REG(INVS) III VIR

Mint of Rome

This coin was Minted well before the invasion, so it must have been brought along with one of the soldiers one would have thought. Although it has some damage, it is a nice coin to find.

311

My 45th item is another silver Denarius of Augustus Caesar and in far better condition than the previous one, but it is dated to 13-14 AD so 40 years or so newer!

The Database report is as follows: A Roman silver Denarius of Augustus dating to 13-14 AD Minted at Lugdunum (Lyon).

Obverse Descr: Laureate head right, retrograde legend.

Obverse Inscr: CAESAR AVGVSTVS DIVI F PATER PATRIAE

Reverse Descr: Livia or Pax seated right holding sceptre and branch, retrograde legend.

Reverse Inscr: PONTIF MAXIM

This very rare coin is the forerunner of the very common denarii of Tiberius with the same reverse.

So it is nice to have something reported by the people who know it to be a rare item.

My 46th item is yet another silver Denarius of Antoninus Pius dated to 139 AD Precisely and minted in Rome.

The PAS Database records it as follows:

A Roman silver Denarius of Antoninus Pius

Obverse Descr: Bare Head right

Obverse Inscr: IMP T AEL CAES HADR ANTONINVS

Reverse Descr: Victory walking right holding wreath and palm.

Reverse Inscr: AVG PIVS P M TR P COS II

In Fine Condition.

Titus Aelius Hadrianus Antoninus Pius—his full name—was emperor from 138-161 AD. He was born into a senatorial family and held various offices during the reign of Hadrian. He married Hadrian's niece Faustina, and Hadrian adopted him as his son and successor shortly before his death. His reign is notable for the peaceful state of the empire, with no major revolts during this time. He died in 156-7 AD of old age, which was a rarity in those times, at the age of 74. He had 4 children (2 of which were adopted).

315

My 47th find of this decade is also Roman, but this time, it is made of bronze. Not many bronze Roman coins come to the surface in a nice condition, so this one is worth showing. It is a Nummus of Crispus dating to 323 AD and minted in Lyon.

The database report says: A Late Roman copper-alloy nummus of Crispus minted in Lyon dated to 323 AD.

Obverse Descr: Laureate, draped and cuirassed bust right.

Obverse Inscr: D N CRISPO NOB CAES

Reverse Descr: Globe set on altar inscribed VOT/IS/XX in three lines: above, three stars.

Reverse Inscr: BEATA TRANQVILLITAS.

Flavius Julius Crispus was born to Constantine I and Minervina in Pola, Istria in 295 AD. He reigned from March 1st 317 to 326 AD, when his father ordered his execution without a trial by cold poison and his name erased from inscriptions.

Very difficult to find a reason though! Must have been bad to upset your own father!

My 48th item is quite a common find to detectorists but they are a bit of our history too. It is a Jews Harp dating to between 1650-1750 AD.

It has different names wherever you go, and is made of different materials too.

This one is made from copper alloy and would have had a reed attached to it to make the sound. The frame was held firmly against the player's parted teeth or lips, using the jaw as a resonator to increase the volume. The jaw must be parted enough for the reed to vibrate freely. The reed is obviously missing from this example. The earliest depiction is from a Chinese drawing from 3rd century BC.

The name, as we know it is misleading and has nothing to do with Jewish people, and it doesn't look like a harp! The name appears earliest in Walter Raleigh's "Discouerie Guiana" in 1596, spelled "Lewes Harp".

Marin Mersenne wrote in 1636, "Although this instrument is used by lackeys and people of lower class, this does not mean it is not worthy of consideration by better minds".

I think it would have been great to listen to them playing them in the fields whilst they worked in the 17th century!

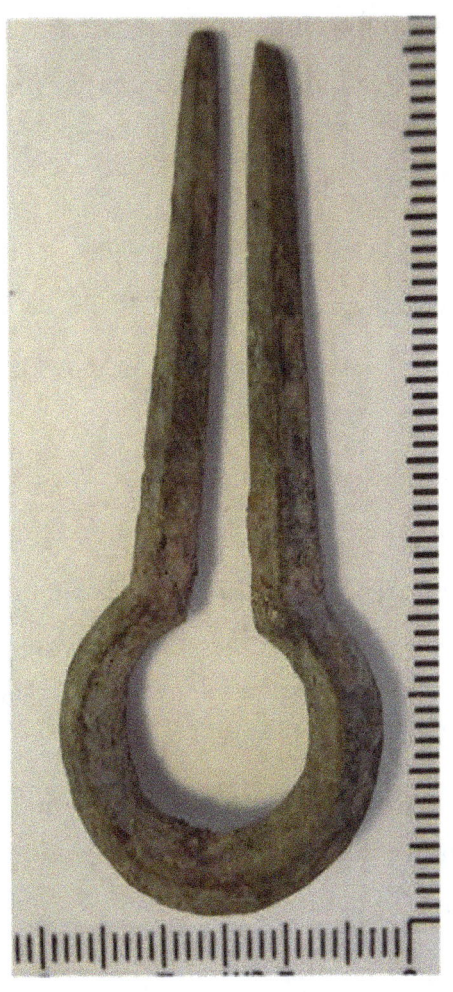

My penultimate find of this decade is a medieval Scottish silver penny of Alexander II dating to 1235-1249 AD.

Minted in Roxburgh.

The report from the Database says: A very worn medieval Scottish silver penny of Alexander II, short cross and stars Coinage.

Obverse Descr: Unclear Bust right.

Obverse Inscr: Illegible

Reverse Descr: Voided short cross with a star in each angle.

Reverse Inscr: ()ARO().

It is a very worn coin, but it is also a coin that we do not normally find this far south. One of the unusual things about these coins is you can find which mint it was from by counting the points of the stars in each quarter. The total will equate to the mint.

Alexander II was King of Scotland from 1214 until his death. He was born in Haddington, East Lothian. Spent time in England and King John Knighted him at Clerkenwell Priory in 1213. Before becoming King of Scotland on the death of his father William I in 1214. He passed away in 1249 AD.

My final item of this decade is another Scottish silver penny this time of Alexander III, dating from 1280-1286 AD. Minted in St Andrews.

The database report states:

Long Cross and Stars type second coinage, solid cross.

Obverse Descr: Crowned Bust Left, sceptre in front, lettering with incurved uprights.

Obverse Inscr: ALEXANDER DEI GRA

Reverse Descr: Long Cross with a star in each angle. Two have six points and a hole in the centre. Two have five points, one has a hole in the centre, 22 points in total.

Reverse inscr: REX SCOTORVM

Alexander was born in Roxburgh in 1241. The only son of Alexander II. He became King at the age of seven in 1249. He married at the age of ten and his wife Margaret (Henry IIIs daughter) was eleven. They had three children, Margaret, Alexander and David. Alexander died after falling from his horse in 1286.

My final thoughts are, if you are not interested in history, or learning more about history then I don't think this hobby of ours will suit you. On the other hand, if you are interested in the past, then this hobby just never fails to provide surprises!

If you are interested in searching the fields within our lovely country, then you need to be patient, you need to be honest with the farmers, you need all the equipment and you need to be prepared to go out in all weathers.

Yes, we are idiots, but it is a great hobby which doesn't stop when you get home. You then have the fun of cleaning your treasures carefully, identifying and if you are like me, logging and photographing all of them, before you take them to your Local Finds Liaison Officer for recording on the UK National Database.

The last ten years have been very fruitful for me in the number of finds made; it could be just luck with the land I was able to get permission to go on, or just the machine I invested in, or both.

I found 1159 coins and 2529 artefacts over these

last ten years, but please remember that buttons and Musket balls are included in the artefacts. Also, bear in mind, I shared all the finds with the farmer.

It was worth it!

I would like to thank our Local Find Liaison Officers in Lincoln for their continued help with the identification and dating all the finds, and for allowing me to use some of their photos and data.

Wikipedia for the use of their information and background knowledge.

Also, my detecting friends within the club who continue to make me smile whenever we are able to have a club dig together and at our monthly meetings.

The landowners too, without which we wouldn't have a hobby and finally, my wife, who doesn't know what it's like to have a husband on a Sunday morning!

You never know; there may be some new finds in the 2020s!

THANK YOU!